BALL
&
CHAIN

The Trouble with Modern Marriage

Nicky Falkof

ff

First published in 2007 by Fusion Press,
a division of Satin Publications Ltd
101 Southwark Street
London SE1 0JF
UK
info@visionpaperbacks.co.uk
www.visionpaperbacks.co.uk
Publisher: Sheena Dewan

A catalogue record for this book is available from the British Library.

ISBN: 978-1-905745-20-3

2 4 6 8 10 9 7 5 3 1

Cover photo: Paul Vozdic/Photonica/Getty Images
Cover and text design by ok?design
Printed and bound in the UK by
Crative Print and Design (Wales), Ebbw Vale

For Brett Goldin

CONTENTS

Acknowledgements

There are a lot of people who aided in the creation of this book, too many to mention them all by name. My thanks must go firstly and most importantly to the many strangers, friends and friends of friends who filled out questionnaires by the truckload and were pestered on the phone or internet, interviewed in drinking establishments across England and pounced on by my Dictaphone every time they mentioned the 'M' word. I was consistently humbled and astounded by the bravery, humour, tenacity, patience and generosity of my respondents, all of whom contributed to this book with no thought of thanks or gain. My appreciation is lasting, and I owe each of you a(nother) pint.

Helen Fisher, Philip Hodson, Frances Lindsay, Christine Northam and Catherine Butler freely gave of their time and expertise. I would not have got much writing done were it not for my cousin Paul Sender and brother Greg Falkof lending me an idyllic location and a car for a quiet retreat. My mother Bev Goldman provided proofreading and patience, among other things harder to quantify. Emily Dubberley, Sara Orning, Samuel Pinney and Sarahs Lewis and Bee offered practical aid, advice, editing and much-needed paid employment. The eternally tolerant Louise Coe, Kate Pollard and Susan Curran made the publishing process far less intimidating. I owe thanks to my lovely, supportive friends Charlotte 'Wilcox' Wilcox (who facilitated, in a way, the whole thing), Rachael Diop, Tammy Sassoon and those others in Brighton, Cape Town, Johannesburg, London, Ireland and Berlin who know, I should hope, who they are.

Author's note

Most of the names in this book, except where specifically requested, are pseudonyms. I owe a debt of gratitude to Stephanie Coontz's excellent *Marriage, A History: How Love Conquered Marriage,*[1] although I hasten to point out that any errors are mine rather than hers. I would also like to engage the maxim of the fabulous and mysterious Nina Farewell, author of *The Unfair Sex: An Exposé of the Human Male for Young Women of All Ages*: 'If some of the statements contained herein seem illogical, or if one chapter appears to contradict another, remember that the author is a member of that sex which is notorious for its inconsistencies. Moreover, life itself is full of contradictions. Ask yourself not "Is it logical?" but rather "Is it true?"'[2]

Introduction

A brief history of marriage

It was the divine Mae West, actress, wit and celebrated diva, who said, 'Marriage is a wonderful institution – but I'm not ready for an institution yet.' We live in a world of gay relationships, cohabitation, single parents and public sexuality, and yet so many of us are still umbilically connected to the dated and depressing idea of marriage. Why this irrelevant urge to justify our relationships by forcing them into uncomfortable legal contracts? Marriage is a relic of religions that few of us really believe in, an antiquated habit that some people are still attached to even though it's lost most of its purpose and meaning. Romantic? Perhaps, but so is waking up every morning and choosing to be with your partner rather than staying put because it's less trouble than getting out. Normal? Possibly, but just because lots of people do something doesn't mean it's right – just look at the Nazis, or the Italian Fascists, or the plague of shoulderpads that blighted the 1980s. I don't dispute that there are many wonderful marriages out there, but those fortunate partnerships hardly justify the continued importance this bloated, out-of-date, choking institution retains for the rest of us.

This book aims to dissect the myths, beliefs, motivations and responses attached to marriage, the social and cultural accessories that make this great white elephant seem so essential to our happiness, when in truth it's been staggering on the edge of functionality for quite some time now.

Tempting as it may be to assume so, I'm no isolated case, nor am I a bitter ageing hag who's failed to find a husband, taken against the idea and decided to put everyone else off it too. Marriage rates all over the world are on the slide as more and more people decide to make their own choices, to live in ways that suit them rather than blindly doing exactly what their parents did. Especially considering that their parents probably got married because that was the only option for a nice boy or girl, and then found themselves battling through ugly divorces when they realised that the person their 19-year-old self thought was just fine did not satisfy the emotional needs of their 49-year-old self.

In February 2007 the BBC reported that wedding rates in the UK were at their lowest since records began. A total of 244,710 people married in 2005, the lowest number since 1896. Weddings were down 10 per cent compared with the previous year.[1] And it's not that people aren't still falling in love and having committed relationships – much to organised religion's dismay, it seems that part of the dip is due to the many couples choosing to live together for ages before they get married, or even to avoid marriage completely and happily maintain their status quo.

News outlets across the United States reported in May 2007 that divorce had reached its lowest level since the 1970s; but rather than signalling a resurgence in traditional marital relations, this was mainly down to the vast number of couples choosing to cohabit and thus breaking up without making a dent in the statistics. The country's divorce rate began climbing in the late 1960s, peaked at 5.3 per 1,000 people in 1981 and has now dropped to 3.6. Keep in mind that these numbers are per

1,000 of all people, including those who are single, married, living with a partner or settled in a polyamorous love quadrangle.

The number of British couples who live together without getting married has gone up ten-fold since 1960 while the marriage rate has dropped nearly 30 per cent in the last 25 years. A spokesperson for Relate, the UK's national relationship counselling service, says, 'We have more people waiting longer and living together for longer before they marry. That's because they want to be sure that they want the same things and that the marriage will be stable and healthy.'

Despite the scare tactics of politicians and religious leaders who insist the drop in marriages is a dangerous blow to the continued stability of polite society,[2] people seem to have an amazing knack for self-regulation. When change comes we work out new answers to the old problems of families and relationships, and make the landscape of our social and emotional lives fit with the differing world and the altered expectations that go with it. No one teaches us how to do this – adaptability is a great human trait, as common and pervasive as the tendency to panic about the end of civilisation as we know it every time a radical paradigm shift occurs. Thirty years ago having children out of wedlock was considered shocking but it's now as common as anything. No one decided this, no one planned or legislated or resolved – it just happened, and eventually our governments and policymakers caught up. And the same has happened with the all-pervasiveness of marriage. Human culture is, at the end of the day, autonomous and organic no matter how many laws and rules we put in place. Despite all the hand-wringing and angst about its inevitable decline, the average family is just getting on with it, finding new ways to form itself with the minimum of fuss or growing pains.

And the demographics are changing to match. In the United Kingdom, for example, the Office of National Statistics predicts that the proportion of unmarried men will rise to 46 per cent by 2031, compared with 35 per cent in 2003. Unmarried women will go from 28 per cent to 39 per cent, with unmarried couples living together going from 2 million in 2003 to 3.8 million in 2031.[3] A drop in marriages will see a consequent drop in divorces, sure to be heartbreaking to certain members of the legal profession, although divorces will rise sharply among the elderly. The proportion of divorcees over 65 is expected to double as more and more people realise they don't have to stay in marriages that make them unhappy. The social and cultural implications of that little marriage certificate retain a disproportionate hold over our inner lives, but the grasp is loosening, freeing us from the restrictive and now largely irrelevant belief that we need to get married in order to be validated, to grow up, to take our places in the world.

Our expectations are changing and society is changing to meet them, no matter how much terror this inspires in church and state and statisticians who are habitually resistant to any progress but the technological. The 21st century may not offer flying cars or teleportation but it's still very different from the 1950s, and our marital habits reflect that change. People all over the world are quietly freeing themselves from the choking bonds of limp, useless convention, of which the assumption that we'll all get married and have 2.4 kids and a DVD player in every room is just one discrete element. This stuff is happening, whether the conservatives like it or not. What remains now is for the rest of you, those still tied to the outdated notion of marriage for one or another reason, to open your eyes a little wider.

This book may seem at first glance like it's merely desperate to tip over a particularly bloated sacred cow, but that's not the whole truth. The whole truth, in fact, is that if you look at that cow in proper lighting it won't be possible to avoid admitting that it isn't a cow at all. Maybe it's a sheep, or a pig, or even a pony (this is going to be something of a recurring theme, so forgive me).

It's an historical truth that the idea of 'traditional' marriage that's held in such high regard and protected from the onslaughts of heathens like myself just isn't that traditional. I attracted a fair amount of vitriol in the research stages of this book from people who were appalled that I'd dare to attack such a venerable and essential institution. When I'd wiped the flecks of spit off my face I usually tried to find out exactly what it was that these incensed traditionalists were trying to defend, and how they defined the 'sacred' institution of marriage. Those who were still willing to speak to me gave the same answer – one man and one woman in love and living happily ever after.

My perceived anti-marriage stance was generally understood as humbugism of the highest order, a cynical anti-romanticism and even, on occasion, a hatred of the very ideas of love and happiness. (None of this is true, by the way. I'm all for love and happiness, just not convinced you need a legal document to get them. Unless one of you is under 16, in which case it really can't hurt.) These responses were also interesting in their insistence on this sort of marriage as 'traditional'. The more outraged assumed I was some sort of anarcho-punk extreme animal rights activist loony lefty type, dedicated to taking down marriage just because it's been around forever. But this commonly held belief in the long provenance of 'traditional' marriage is just another of the pleasant fictions that have accrued around the matrimonial imperative over the years.

Any historian will confirm that the love-based 'man in the office/woman in the kitchen' marriages of the 1950s were a cultural and historical anomaly. The spread of popular culture, the injection of television into homes and the post-war prosperity of the United States all combined to make sure that sitcom marriages like those seen in *Happy Days* seemed, suddenly, like the norm, when in fact this 'traditional' marriage to which our culture still harks back is barely a century old.

In *Little Shop of Horrors*, the 1986 film based on the popular gothic-shlock musical, the trashy-with-a-heart-of-gold heroine Audrey dreams of her emancipation from Steve Martin's sadistic dentist in favour of a picture-perfect suburban life with Rick Moranis' nerdy Seymour. Her fantasy sequence involves spinning around a postcard house with the ubiquitous white picket fence, patting her two cute kids on the head and grinning like a primary school art teacher on acid. She wants to 'cook like Betty Crocker and look like Donna Reed' as she enjoys 'a washer and a dryer and an ironing machine', in between their TV dinners and 'bedtime 9.15'. It's a perfectly excessive parody of the ultimate 1950s marital fancy, with the husband as Man and the wife as his Lady. Sweet, innocuous, naïve and hopeless, Audrey's 'Somewhere that's green' is a place that only ever existed in the popular imagination.

Even during the so-called 'long decade' of the 1950s, the golden era of conservative love-based marriage when the divorce rate and average marital age both dropped, this was a dearly held fantasy, one that proved the dark days of the Second World War were over and the Future had well and truly arrived (robot cars being, of course, only just around the corner). It would be disingenuous to suggest that all marriages in the 1950s were really this idyllic, but nonetheless it seems to have been a common goal, and housewifery a perfectly acceptable end point for young women.

Although this vision of harmonious complicity between Man and Wife sneaked its way into the popular consciousness, it was never going to last. The 1960s came along with their -isms, long hair, birth control and radicalisation, and suddenly 'traditional' marriage was under threat.

The idea that women should be completely satisfied with their roles as wife and mother first became an issue for public debate in 1963, when feminist Betty Friedan published her hugely influential book *The Feminine Mystique.*[4] Friedan posited the notion on a grand scale that women were unfulfilled, frustrated and stuck in the home, providing mothering to husbands who'd come back from the war, sublimating their desires and abilities for the greater good of the family. When she died in February 2006, her *New York Times* obituary said:

> With its impassioned yet clear-eyed analysis of the issues that affected women's lives in the decades after World War II – including enforced domesticity, limited career prospects and, as chronicled in later editions, the campaign for legalised abortion – *The Feminine Mystique* is widely regarded as one of the most influential non-fiction books of the 20th century.[5]

Women being unsatisfied with a life lived only in the home hardly seems today like a radical notion, and the far-reaching effect of Friedan's thesis helps to prove just how untouchable the institution of traditional marriage was. But the fast-forgotten fact was that it had never been traditional. It was rare before the developing prosperity of the 20th century for a working-class man to be the sole breadwinner: wives generally worked, possibly behind the scenes but nonetheless involved. They'd engage in the family business to some extent, seldom as its public face but generally providing support and input that increased the family's earnings and chance of survival. The image of the middle-class 'little woman' as a happy home-maker with no economic contribution to the marriage, that icon that 1960s and 1970s feminism endangered, was actually as new and shiny as the many appliances in her kitchen.

Historians do, as I've said, agree that the 1950s love match was a new phenomenon rather than a smooth continuation of the custom of centuries, as most of our current popular culture and belief systems imply. But there is far more to the complicated history of marital relations than this. In her exhaustive survey of the subject, *Marriage, A History: How Love Conquered Marriage*, historian Stephanie Coontz argues convincingly that 1950s marriage was not an isolated aberration but the culmination of a project that began in the 18th century to integrate love into marriage, peaking in the 1950s with what we've now come to believe is 'traditional' marriage.

'In the 1970s, when the inherent instability of the love-based marriage reasserted itself, millions of people were taken completely by surprise,' she writes. 'Having lost any collective memory of the convulsions that occurred when the love match was first introduced . . . they could not understand why this kind of marriage, which they thought had prevailed for thousands of years, was being abandoned by the younger generation.'[6] Not only was love as the basis of marriage a new and radical idea, the assumption that one should be free to choose one's spouse based on taste and emotion only began to be acceptable in fairly recent history, and then only in Western Europe and North America as a general rule. Coontz writes:

> Until the late 18th century, most societies around the world saw marriage as far too vital an economic and political institution to be left entirely to the free choice of the two individuals involved, especially if they were going to base their decision on something as unreasoning and transitory as love.[7]

Marriage, until the last few hundred years, was not about individual happiness but about group survival. Children would be married off by their parents in a careful bid to maximise the potential of the union: more land, stronger allies, closer ties with neighbours, alliances to families who shared the same craft, all of these advantages would be considered by the group's ruling parties when a youth reached marriageable age – or even before. Examples abound of children being betrothed to each other before they were old enough to walk because the match would be to the advantage of both families when it finally came about. This is about as far removed from our current starry-eyed interpretation of marriage as it's possible to be. Love existed, all right, but it had no place in the social and political motivation behind a decent marriage, nor was it considered a good enough reason to take a step that had such far-reaching implications for oneself and one's clan. The difference between survival and starvation could be made in a clever marriage and a cunning alliance of in-laws.

Marriage has taken many forms in the course of human history, some of them barely related to our idealised version of the traditional. According to Martin Whyte, a professor of sociology at Harvard and the author of *Dating, Mating and Marriage*,[8] early reports from missionaries, explorers and anthropologists suggest that only 20 to 35 per cent of pre-industrial societies were monogamous, less than 1 per cent polyandrous, and the rest polygynous. 'Monogamy as the dominant and mandated pattern is of more recent vintage historically,' he says.

Polygamy, being married to more than one person, was particularly common and still exists in certain cultures today. Joseph Smith, one of the founders of Mormonism, practised a form of polygamy – or more properly polygyny, since it only ever involved a single man and many wives – called plural marriage. The official Mormon church bowed to the US Government's pressure in 1890 and swore off the practice, with Mormonism now a respected global faith. But fundamentalist schisms angry at the government's attempt to regulate their socio-sexual lives broke away from the central church to start their own closed communities, mostly in Utah and parts of Canada, where the 'sacred doctrine' of plural marriage is unanimous even today. Girls in their early teens are routinely married off to multiple-wived patriarchs in their 60s.[9]

In ancient China it was perfectly acceptable for a man to marry his wife with all due ceremony and then take concubines when he could afford them. In the new prosperous 21st-century China a married businessmen will often have an *ernai* – a sexually servicing second wife, the modern version of a concubine, a kept woman whose beauty and lifestyle are testament to her master's taste and wealth. Polyandry – a woman having many husbands – is far less frequent than its opposite but was the standard for certain tribes, among them the Canadian Inuit (the practice declined sharply with the introduction of Christian mores into their civilisation).

In the *Mahabharata*, the epic Sanskrit poem that is one of the jewels of classical Indian culture, the Pandava prince Arjuna, disguised as a Brahmin, wins the hand of the princess Draupadi. A complicated plot twist ensues and to save his mother's honour he must share her with his four brothers, so she becomes a common wife to them all.

Few societies have permitted group marriage (marriage between many couples), but it has happened, notably in Utopian communities like the Native American Oneida tribe.

Nambudiri Brahmin in India practise henogamy, in which only the eldest son in each family can marry. Catholic nuns are the brides of Jesus, married for all intents and purposes to their God. Levirate marriage, common among central Asian nomads and in central and southern Africa as well as in the Old Testament, was the marriage of a widow to her husband's brother in order to continue the late husband's line. The brother often had a wife of his own already, so the bereaved woman was taken into a family grouping. Sororate marriage, also common among Inuit, sees a man marrying or having sex with his wife's sister, usually if the wife has died or been proven infertile. Chinese 'ghost marriages' saw a young person married off to the dead son or daughter of another family in order to forge close ties with them. In the 20th century some young women began to actively choose these marriages so their families could have the benefit of in-laws while they retained their independence.

For all the crowing about 'traditional' marriage that goes on within religious and cultural debates, for all the panicking about the crisis in marriage engendered by immorality, short skirts and rock 'n' roll, this venerated institution has sometimes taken forms that would shock and appal the traditionalists – yet they're as valid a part of human history as mum, dad, John, Jane and Spot.

Stephanie Coontz explains the struggle of academics to come up with a clear definition of the term. In 1949 the respected American anthropologist George Peter Murdoch called it a 'universal institution that involves a man and a woman living together, engaging in sexual activity and cooperating economically'. But what about married couples who don't live together, like the Ashanti of Ghana? Nope, back to the drawing board. The Royal Anthropological Institute of Great Britain and Ireland gave it a go with 'a union between a man and a woman such that children born to the woman are the recognised legitimate offspring of both partners'. But this cancels out the societies that recognised male-male marriage, or marriages of political advantage where the woman is barren or too old to bear children. In the late 1950s, British anthropologist Edmund Leach suggested that marriage should be seen as being more about regulating property than about raising children, but in some societies inheritance rights have nothing to do with marriage. Suzanne Frayser came up with 'a relationship within which a society socially approves and encourages sexual intercourse and the birth of children'.[10] But all that really does is define marriage by its most common features, which doesn't help us to understand what functions it performs or what it means, and ignores the elements of social cohesion and group development that seem fundamental to the whole idea.

We can see from this brief survey that the question of what marriage really is isn't as black and white as all that, nor are the answers to questions about its use and validity as simple as some would have us imagine. It is neither a given nor an uncomplicated essential, but rather a complex issue that defies the simplistic 'it is what it is' approach of political and religious conservatives, for whom the protection of this 'venerable' institution outweighs all considerations of balance. That said, for the duration of this book I shall focus mainly on marital traditions from Western Europe and North America, and the countries and communities most influenced by them. Marriage itself is too vast, too varied, too multi-faceted to take on all at once.

Marriage pre-dates the world's current major religions, although they have co-opted it as a duty and holy sacrament, and it has been found in one form or another in every recorded human culture but one.[11] Strange as it may seem for a pair bonding that appears to be intrinsically about a couple, marriage was originally a group concern: early humans found that pairing people off in units of two worked toward the greater good of the group. The man would go out hunting and face the possibility of returning empty-handed while the woman would gather food from the surrounding area and ensure there was something to keep everyone alive if he failed. Working together as a pair doubled the chances of survival for both them and their offspring, and when these couples lived together in groups their pairings created stronger bonds between in-laws, which in turn made continued existence more likely.

While anthropologists can only speculate when, where and how formalised marriage began, the act of joining together to rear children and pool resources is as old as the species – because it was essential. There was no other way to live. As civilisation progressed, formal coupling became a political tool for the advancement of the wealthy and titled and an economic tool for the survival of the working class. Marriage had more to do with increasing a labour force, gaining useful in-laws and having children than it did with personal satisfaction and happiness. The practice of providing dowries and bride prices was common all over the world. In such circumstances, where parents' fortunes were involved and a child's marriage was an investment, it would hardly make sense to leave these decisions up to the wilful caprice of youngsters. Farms and businesses could not usually be run alone so marrying someone provided you with a co-worker you didn't need to pay, whose commitment was as strong as your own. Wives toiled alongside their husbands to keep the family alive.

In Ancient Greece love was honoured and marriage was common but they were seldom found together. The love that was lauded was of the 'noble' variety that only existed between two men, whereas marriage was functional and served a purpose. Roman law allowed for prostitution, the keeping of concubines and a master's sexual access to his slaves, alongside the norms of 'monogamous' marriage. Royals in Ancient Egypt, Hawaii and the Inca lands of South America were expected to marry their siblings, with a brother-sister marital pair securing the throne and the succession.

In sixth-century Europe Christianity held sway and polygamy was not permitted, but this didn't stop the Germanic warlord Clothar from marrying four strategically useful women, including his dead brother's wife, her sister and the daughter of a captured king. Aristocrats in 12th-century

Europe believed that love was impossible within marriages, which were generally arranged to the benefit of all before the couple had even met. In 1344 the lord of a Black Forest manor took his villagers' marital lives literally into his own hands, decreeing that all unmarried tenants, even widows and widowers, must wed someone of his choosing. Around the same time, peasants wishing to marry someone of their own choice were forced to pay a fee.

Jump to the New World, and in the United States in the late 1600s it was considered unseemly for a husband and wife to love each other too much. A Virginia colonist describes a woman as 'more fond of her husband perhaps than the politeness of the day allows'. Ministers actually warned people against loving their spouses too much, and women were castigated for calling their husbands by pet names because this diminished a man's authority.

But by the late 18th century love was gaining ground as a reason for marriage, and English campaigners were bemoaning women's need to enter loveless marriages in order to survive economically. This was also the time when women, who had always been perceived as the lustier, more sexual gender, suddenly metamorphosed into a vision of virginal purity, as illustrated by Queen Victoria's break with the traditional red to wed her consort in pure white lace. This paved the way for the sexual repression of the high Victorians, who took their obsessive decency so far that table legs had to be covered because they were considered obscene. This in turn created the endemic hysteria that plagued upper- and middle-class women during the Freud years at the dawning of the 20th century. Freud and an open academic dialogue about sex combined with the new focus on love to bring men and women together socially. Soon kids were dating all over the show and the idea of marrying for anything *but* love seemed insane and inhumane.

Two wars and a pop culture explosion later, and the 1950s happened in a blur of Formica, TV dinners and progress, creating an idealised image of the strictly gendered love marriage. It's since passed into the general imagination as 'tradition', something that's always been there and is currently under threat. But it hasn't.

It seems to me that when we or our leaders lionise marriage and the nuclear family, we are doing so in the blind hope that a return to these values will also return us to the 'good old days' of the 1950s, a period of prosperity and progress in the United States and the moment when television initiated the increased mass export of its popular culture, making it seem in retrospect like a golden age for the entire Western world. But we're going about it the wrong way, hoping that 'traditional' marriage will be a cause rather than a consequence of contentment and affluence. This situation is a lot like the cargo cults that sprang up in New Guinea and Melanesia after the Second World War. US soldiers landed on these Pacific islands while fighting the Japanese, and with them came air-dropped cargo packages of clothing, medicine and canned food, untold luxuries for islanders who had never even seen Europeans before. When the war ended so did the cargo drops, and a fascinating religion sprang up whereby the islanders attempted to imitate what they'd seen the US soldiers do to inspire the gods to continue to shower munificence on them from the skies. They carved headphones from wood, made replica planes out of straw, lit up the empty runways with signal fires.

We 'sophisticated' Westerners are falling victim to a similar urge. We're trying to recreate the conditions of plenty to tempt plenty back. We assume that if we can return marriage to the unambiguous state of perfection it seemed to have back then, everything else will follow it and we'll go back to a halcyon period of happiness and stability that really only happened in

TV-land and the popular imagination. We are pining for the structure of an imaginary golden age in the hopes that it will somehow recreate the substance.

The homemaker/provider/two kids model is a beautiful daydream (for some; for others it's the ultimate nightmare) that never really was, and definitely never really was traditional. We're sighing over a moment that didn't happen.

In the 1990s sociologist Amy Kaler interviewed people in a region of southern Africa where divorce had long been common.[12] Her respondents bewailed the uncertain state of marriage, insisting that all this trouble was new to their generation. But when she examined oral histories from the same culture she found that 50 years before, these same people's grandparents were lamenting the state of their own marriages and insisting that their parents hadn't had these problems. Assuming that marriage was always easier in the past seems to be a fixed habit of humanity. The golden age we're harking back to just didn't exist; the venerable institution so deeply threatened by change and unconventional behaviour has, in truth, always been at risk.

Coontz writes, 'Probably the single most important function of marriage through most of history, although it is almost completely eclipsed today, was its role in establishing cooperative relationships between families and communities.'[13] Marriage kept families together and helped them survive. It organised people and society and goods, much the way government does today. Love was disruptive because it made people withdraw into coupledom instead of committing to the wider group. But the act of marriage performs none of these functions today, and the mainstream emphasis is on couples or on the nuclear family. The marriage of one's child provides no benefits for parents or relatives except the dubious joy of seeing their offspring prance about in needlessly expensive outfits. The religious imperative to marry in order to keep sexuality between husband and wife is like shutting the stable door long after the horse has bolted in a world where teen pregnancy is rife, young girls walk around with Playboy bunnies emblazoned on their undeveloped chests and being a stripper is a viable life choice.

In our culture of rampant porn-style sexiness, where Paris Hilton's celebrity is ramped up 200 per cent by a home video that shows her looking incredibly bored while having mediocre sex, the old-fashioned morality that marriage once supported is an anachronism and an irrelevance, as borne out by the statistical failure of George W Bush's government's ridiculous attempt to teach abstinence until marriage rather than contraception and condom usage.[14] You don't even need to be married to have kids, as the many single birth and adoptive parents around the world prove every day. Illegitimacy is no longer a blight on a child's future, so there's no need to marry the first available candidate as soon as you find out you're knocked up. It's unlikely that a modern marriage will occur for political gain or for an economic alliance – although the rich marrying the rich is always going to be standard – and unless you're a member of a royal family you probably won't ruin anyone else's life but your own by marrying someone inappropriate.[15] So why do we do it? Why bother? Because it's romantic? You could just make each other breakfast in bed, you know.

Philip Hodson is a writer, psychotherapist and fellow of the British Association for Counselling and Psychotherapy who specialises in marriage and relationship counselling. 'Marriage is in decline,' he says.

> Cohabitation is aggressively taking over. People are coming to a privatisation of their relationships – we don't see why the church or state should tell us who to be intimate with. Marriage

> was originally about witnessing, about your friends and neighbours seeing who you were paired with so that a father could be sure which were his children. There are a lot more anthropological and sociological bases, of course, but that was one of the primary ones – so you'd be able to leave your flock of sheep to the rightful heir. And that just isn't an issue anymore. We've come to stage where the cult of individualism and rights means that relationships are private (whether this is a good thing or a bad thing for society is another question). There is an enormous panic about the 'crisis' in marriage that is completely out of proportion because the family is surviving just fine, in different permutations. Not marrying means that people can't classify you as easily and they have to think about how to relate to you and refer to you, which is a good thing. Choice is healthy. Conventional matrimony is often a recipe for a coma – and I say that as a marriage counsellor.[16]

People get married, like people do most things, for a whole variety of reasons. Unfortunately for those left wallowing in post-matrimonial chaos they're often not the right reasons. 'But wait!' I hear you bellow from the cheap seats at the back. 'Right? What's this talk of *right*? Who are you to decide what's right?' Fortunately it isn't as black and white as all that. There is indeed a right reason for every decision – but that reason depends entirely on the person making the decision. Your emotional, cultural and social make-up are paramount; that elusive sprite that's sometimes called personality and sometimes character dictates what will work for each of us and what most patently will not. You can be damned sure that what makes your best friend happy may well be disastrous for you, no matter how much you have in common and how great it would be to keep doing things together like you did when you were ten.

If there's a common thread to these enlivening, uplifting and healthy decisions then it's all to do with how particular they are. It's about how careful we are to make choices that are really appropriate for us rather than following the herd, doing what we think needs to be done or attempting to fill an emotional gap with the relationship equivalent of that sub-jam substance that supermarkets shovel into the middle of value-pack donuts.

Why do we do what we do? Why do we make the choices that we make? If, that is, we have the self-awareness to really make choices at all rather than falling floppily into the path of least resistance. They say the road to hell is paved with good intentions, but there's a fair whack of laziness, carelessness and fear lurking around that address too. Many of us wander around blindfolded, heads in the sand, blithely doing whatever we see other people doing so we don't have to make difficult decisions or take complicated positions.

A lot of marriages – and shockingly, a lot of children – are like bad tattoos. It was late, you were a bit drunk, everyone else was getting one, it was a bonding thing, you thought it would be fun. When you wake up on Monday morning with a shabbily sketched skull and crossbones on your bicep or a wonky 'tribal' stamp across your arse it's hard to believe that the damn thing will be there forever, for the rest of your life, a visual reminder of how thoughtless you were and how little you valued the integrity of your body. Unless, of course, you get it removed with expensive and excruciating laser treatments, and even then you'll always have the scar to keep you wary.

There's a reason that religious and civil ceremonies persist in making us say that we take our spouses for life; if your plans or desires or projected futures are different, then just don't bloody get married. Life is a long time. Having a rose on your left breast might well seem sexy, edgy and individual when you're

23, but when you're 53 it'll be saggy and illegible. Like marriages, there are a lot of really good tattoos out there. Some people get body art because they want to grow with it, because they're ready for the long-term commitment it entails, because they've considered the implications and thought about the design for months and found someone sympathetic to do it for them. Others, however, can't imagine ever being 53, so they merrily bounce into the marital equivalent of Joe's Bargain Tat Store – All Ages Catered For when they've had a few too many on a Friday night, sniggering at the very idea of their future middle-aged selves and making casual, destructive choices that will echo across the fabric of their lives.

A survey reported in the *Sun* newspaper in the UK in April 2007 claimed that 25 per cent of married people wished they hadn't got married, while 15 per cent of those had doubts even as they walked down the aisle. With 560,000 due to marry in the UK in 2007, that's 84,000 people who are already unhappy with their decisions or will be soon. Researcher John Sewell said, 'People tie the knot for all sorts of reasons. But many aren't sure they want to.' Some claimed love was their motivating factor, some claimed family pressure, some just wanted to get the presents.[17]

Each of the following chapters in this book corresponds to one of the most common reasons for getting married that cropped up during my interviews. None of them satisfied me – but perhaps you'll be less demanding. From soft-focus popcorn romanticism to a pathological terror of standing out from the crowd, they're all there in glorious Technicolor. There are sad stories, happy stories and downright ridiculous stories. There are no easy answers; but then life doesn't tend to have those. Writing this book made me interrogate my assumptions, my motivations and my belief systems, more than once. I hope reading it will do the same for you.

Chapter One

'We were in love'

Ah, love. Be still my beating heart. No, I mean it, be still. Oh for crying out loud . . . Whoever suggested that love was always a good thing was clearly delusional. Or in love. As I write these words (it is, poignantly, Valentine's Day) I'm experiencing a deep sense of relief that my mind is my own; that I'm not waiting for someone to call, that I can concentrate on getting things done rather than lazing around languidly and sighing at three-minute intervals or rushing about like a puppy on a sugar high, waxing areas of my body I only recently realised I had.

Love ain't anything like the pop songs claim. Take, for example, the extensive romantic canon of emotional propagandist and all-around shouty lady Celine Dion. In 'Because you loved me' she credits her lover's presence with her entire existence. In the creatively titled 'I love you' she promises to stay with him forever and ever and ever (eventual physical decrepitude and death, one surmises, not withstanding). In 'Love can move mountains' she extols the possibilities of her emotional range and the miracles it can accomplish. Sorry to have to bust your bubble, honey, but no, it can't. Love may well make you very happy for a while but it's not going to be moving anything, least of all geological features. Pulp, the seminal UK indie band, did a far better job of capturing the first overwhelming rush of teenage experience in their 'F.E.E.L.I.N.G. C.A.L.L.E.D. L.O.V.E', a poignant evocation of the messy, inconvenient and downright disturbing experience of having your comfortable life rattled to bits by a sudden infatuation.

Love is indeed dirtier, and more complicated, than our culture would have us believe. Force-fed a sickening diet of celebrity romances, pop music pining and nauseating filmic fare, it's no wonder we've become obsessed with the idea of love, to the point where it's seen as a right rather than a privilege, and those who don't have it are pitied. (Even so, I'd bet you good money that some of those who do are faking. That revolting couple cooing in the corner? He wishes he was watching the game with his friends, she'd rather be parked in front of *Grey's Anatomy* but she's too embarrassed to tell him she likes it.)

I'm not suggesting that love doesn't exist or even that it isn't important; what I *am* suggesting is that the degree of cultural weight it carries in the early 21st century is disproportionate. We're living for love, and making decisions based on it too, when all too often that feeling – no matter how uplifting – is nowhere close to permanent, and said goodbye to its old friend reason a long time ago. And as grounds for a marriage it quite regularly does not hold up to scrutiny, particularly in those first mad flushes that make us lose our heads. It's no wonder that so many marriages fail when we expect miracles from our spouses. According to a recent study, 70 per cent of Americans think the purpose of marriage is something other than having children, with most expecting their husband or wife to somehow, miraculously, Make Them Happy. Some go further and assume that if they're not happy they must have picked the wrong person, that the fault is with their partner, whose duty it is to improve their lives.[1]

If love is your justification for making a formal and lifetime commitment then it needs to be a certain kind of love: tempered, moderate, conscious, aware, intelligent, respectful, rather than hyped, hysterical, hectic. And since this is not the type of love we see glorified in our popular culture, a culture that values drama *über alles*, this is not the type of love that most people strive for. Your average Joe or Jane on the street wants to be swept off his or her feet, not discover a mutual passion for Scrabble. As we saw in the Introduction, love as a reason for marriage is another one of those wacky modern inventions, like cars and hairdryers and deep fat fryers, that we think we couldn't live without. But humans managed remarkably well marrying for economic or political reasons for a remarkably long time. This is not to suggest that the idea of love was, like our current image of Santa Claus, invented in the early 20th century.[2] Love has a lush and gorgeous romantic history. It's not, however, a history necessarily conducive to long-term commitment and settling down to share a mortgage.

Romantic love in European history

Courtly love, one of the few historical examples that glorified this difficult emotion as much as the romcom-obsessed late 20th century, was a social invention of the Middle Ages that flourished in Europe for about a century from the mid-1100s. The Dark Ages were characterised by practicality and communal thinking, the best way to survive the Barbarian invasions that kept Europe in a state of terror. After the year 1000, when the invasions petered out and the Viking raids stopped, a period of relative peace descended and people had the freedom again to discover themselves as individuals rather than prioritising the survival of their cultural groupings. Once more the arts began to flourish, with poetry and music becoming widespread outside the closed walls of the monasteries. And along with these creative urges came a new romantic sensibility.

The French regions of Provence, Aquitaine, Champagne and Burgundy were a fertile breeding ground for the reinvention of love, expressed by the lyric poetry of the troubadours and trouveres of this area. The magnificent Eleanor of Aquitaine, one of the most powerful female figures of the Middle Ages, was thought to have brought the ideal with her during her turns as Queen Consort of first France then England. She probably saw it as a way to keep her scheming courtiers occupied with something other than plotting her downfall. Eleanor's daughter, Countess Marie de Champagne, later commissioned an ecclesiastical scholar named Andreas Capellanus to write a treatise on love. Called *De arte honeste amandi* (*The Art of Honest Love*, commonly known as *The Art of Courtly Love*), it became almost a guidebook to the notion of this type of romance.

The term itself, *amour courtois*, was invented by French medieval scholar Gaston Paris and not used until 1883. It was, Paris explained, about a man's idolising the object of his desire. The lover accepts that his mistress is independent and tries to become worthy of her by acting bravely and performing whatever noble deeds she might require. In an era when marriage was usually arranged for less than romantic reasons, courtly love tended to fix on extramarital affairs. Definitions vary from writer to writer (most of these writers were male, meaning we have little information on how women at the time felt about being elevated onto such high pedestals), but there were certain standards that stretched across all forms and variants.

Sexual love between men and women is splendid and worth striving for. Love ennobles both lover and beloved. Because it is an ethical and aesthetic pursuit, sexual love is not about mere physical urges. Love is involved in courtesy and courtship but need have nothing to do with marriage. Love is an intense and passionate relationship that establishes a 'holy oneness' between man and woman.[3] Courtly love was a strange mix of the sexual and the spiritual. While it never denied the physical attraction of the lover – there is an abundance of surviving lyrics that detail the glory of the lady's skin, eyes and hair – this tradition also imbued relations between men and women with an almost mystical significance, and the ability to allow the lover to transcend the bounds of human endeavour.

The Roman Catholic Church did not approve of courtly love as it inspired men to give their wholehearted devotion to beautiful women rather than to Christ. Lust is one of the seven deadly sins, and marriage is the only way to avoid it. It was the Apostle Paul who said, in I Corinthians 7:9, 'Let them marry, for it is better to marry than to burn.' Marriage, in the eyes of the Church, was a sacrament and a duty within which procreation occurred, and that was the only acceptable outlet for sexuality. Spouses were supposed to work alongside each other, prop up the state, grow produce and rear families. All this over-emotional sighing about the beauty of a woman's breast or the majesty of her gaze didn't fit too well in the austere Catholic tradition, which reserved the majority of a citizen's emotional life for his relationship with God.

By the start of the 13th century the courtly tradition was outlawed as heretical. Although driven underground the romantic ideals of love continued to be felt across European culture, from the chivalrous insistence on an idealised view of women to the *comic fabliaux*, amusing tales of cuckolded husbands, and more literary romantic fables like the tragic story of Tristan and Iseult all the way up to Miguel de Cervantes' classic tragicomedy *Don Quixote*, first published in 1605.

Hardly a recipe for farting in bed, doing the dishes together and arguing about money, courtly love involved a glorification of the desired object to an almost god-like status of unmarred – and definitely unmarried – perfection, radically different from modern expectations of a life shared completely. Far from asking her husband to pick up her Tampax in the weekly shop, the recipient of a noble's courtly love would be more likely to swoon and faint away if anything so base were alluded to.

Stories, tales and legends

If we were to judge by the profusion of romantic prattling throughout the records of human existence we'd probably assume that the union of man and woman in goo-goo-eyed adoration has always been one of civilisation's driving forces, but the truths of these tales are often far less emotive than they seem. Let's look at one of history's great love stories, immortalised forever in the smoky nightclub tune 'Fever'.

Pocahontas was a Native American princess, beloved daughter of Powhatan, the powerful chief of the Algonquian Indians in the Tidewater region of Virginia. She was born around 1595 and was about 12 years old when she met Captain John Smith in May 1607, when the English landed at what is now Jamestown. Their meeting is often cited as a legendary example of love at first sight. In December of that year Smith led an expedition into the interior, where he was taken prisoner and eventually brought to the residence of Pocahontas' father. The story as Smith related it was that he was first welcomed and then attacked, grabbed and laid on flat rocks while the chief's warriors stood over him with clubs, ready to beat him to death. Suddenly, like a force of nature, a little girl rushed in and took Smith's 'head in her arms and laid her owne upon his to save him from death'. She pulled him to his feet, whereupon he was kissed by the chief and adopted as a son or subordinate chief.

A heart-warming story of true love and a father bowing to his headstrong daughter's wishes? Er, not quite. Despite Smith's subsequent romanticising of the situation it's now generally accepted that the mock 'execution and salvation' ceremony was a traditional one for a powerful newcomer to the tribe, and Pocahontas' actions were in all likelihood a pre-planned element of an important Algonquian ritual. Although the pair later became close, they were not, as far as history knows, romantically involved. Indeed, many years later when the now Christian and married Pocahontas was brought to England, she met her old friend and publicly called him 'father' – an odd reaction to the alleged love of her life.

Love has, too, a great history in literature.[4] Shakespeare's *Anthony and Cleopatra* is generally accepted as a glorious tragedy based on the true story of a couple who risked everything for love. The reality is less romantic but considerably more interesting. Just 17 when she ascended the throne of Egypt and became locked in a mortal power struggle with her brother's supporters, the young Cleopatra was canny and raised in political intrigues. She knew that getting the might of Rome on her side could only be a good thing. Whether she convinced Julius Caesar to support her by seducing him with her nubile body or whether it was a mutually beneficial political arrangement, none can say – although it does seem more likely that the great conqueror of Europe was not blinded to his own advantage by the physical charms of an exotic girl.

After Caesar's murder Cleopatra waited to see which way the wind would blow before committing herself to Anthony. The ancient poet Plutarch relates how Anthony fell instantly in love with her after she sailed to meet him dressed as the Goddess of Love. But again, it seems that this earth-shaking man, possibly the next leader of Rome, had motivations other than his genitals for signing up to Cleopatra's crusade. Cleopatra had borne

Caesar a son, Caesarion, who had been acknowledged by the Emperor and was thus potentially in line for the throne ahead of Anthony's bitter rival, Caesar's adopted son Octavian. Since Caesarion was too young to rule in Rome, Anthony graciously offered to become regent for the boy.

Anthony put aside his Roman wife, Octavian's sister Octavia, and claimed the crown of Rome on behalf of Cleopatra's son, burning his bridges and staking everything on beating the enraged Octavian's armies. When this gamble failed and the battle was lost, both Anthony and Cleopatra committed suicide rather than face being paraded through the streets of Rome as prisoners. Whether there was a true romantic passion between them or not, Anthony's championing of his Egyptian lover was more a risky play for ultimate power than a reckless romantic gesture. Another example of a grand, passionate love that actually conceals far more pragmatism than we're led to believe.

On the subject of Shakespeare, acknowledged as the English language's greatest dramatist and love poet, there are doubts as to how the man himself arranged his romantic life. His famous sonnets were written about two recurrent objects: the Fair Youth and the Dark Lady. In his 1985 book *Such Is My Love*, critic Joseph Pequigney argues convincingly that the poet's love for the Youth is unmistakably homoerotic, and that prudery and homophobia have prevented mainstream scholars from acknowledging the obvious.[5] Whether or not Shakespeare was gay is a question best left to the legions of frothy-mouthed academics who populate the two sides of this heated debate. What is clear, though, is that neither of these two lovers much resembles Anne Hathaway, whom he married in 1582.

There is even some doubt as to whether this older woman was the one poor Will actually wanted to be with. Recordings in the Episcopal register reveal that he married Anne Hathaway on 28 November in Stratford-upon-Avon; but the same source shows that he registered his intention to marry one Anne Whatley the day before, in nearby Temple Grafton. Either these two women were the same and historians are the victims of a clerical error, or another man shared the playwright's name and then vanished from the records forever after getting married, or the Anne that Shakespeare loved and the one he married were different. In either case we know that Hathaway was pregnant before the marriage and that it was, in all likelihood, of the shotgun variety.

The Bard historically admitted to various infidelities and indiscretions. Whether the sonnets' objects were real lovers, imagined ciphers or idols admired from afar, it seems clear that this greatest poet of love had no difficulty projecting the mysteries of romance far outside the cloistered bonds of marriage.

The French Emperor Napoleon and his first wife Josephine are often cited as an example of a touching romantic marriage. While historians agree that the young Corsican soldier fell hard for the entrancing older widow, it seems – if we can examine history from such a whimsical standpoint – to have been more like a youthful obsession than the star-crossed romance it's often painted as. Witness the evidence.

Widowed after her husband was guillotined in 1794 and having narrowly escaped a political death herself, the beautiful Marie Josèphe Rose de Beauharnais became mistress to a number of political figures. It was during this time that she met General Bonaparte, six years her junior, who almost immediately became infatuated with her. It's suggested that one of her lovers, the politician Paul Francois Jean Nicolas Barras, actively encouraged her affair with the upcoming young hero because her financial habits were draining him dry.

From the start of their involvement Napoleon showered her with florid love letters, many of which are still in existence.

(Very few remain from her to him, either because they've been lost or because they were never written.) They were married in 1796 and Napoleon left to lead the French campaign in Italy soon after. The letters continued, but it seems clear that Josephine was hardly matching the devotion of her soldier, as she quickly embarked on an affair with high-society playboy Hippolyte Charles. Napoleon was incensed and soon took his own mistress, Pauline Bellisle Foures, the wife of a junior officer.

This seems to have marked a turning point in the future emperor's temporary adoration of his feckless wife. While no other lovers of Josephine's are recorded, Napoleon was famous for his affairs. A crisis blew up in their marriage in 1804 when Josephine caught her 'devoted' husband in the bedroom of her maid, and he threatened to divorce her for not producing an heir, but the wounds were papered over and the pair crowned Emperor and Empress the same year. The marriage limped on for a few more years until finally, in January 1810, it was acknowledged that Josephine would never bear Napoleon a child and they divorced. A scant two months later he was married by proxy to Marie Louise of Austria.

It is, of course, impossible to say what was going on in the heads and emotional lives of these long-distant historical players. We cannot say whether Napoleon 'truly' loved his wife, whether her initial betrayal caused his subsequent lack of faith, or whether his youthful infatuation with an older woman was subtly put aside once he became emperor in favour of a more advantageous marriage to someone who matched his own increased stature. (Marie Louise did, by the way, produce the requisite heir, Napoleon III of France.) What we can say for sure, though, is what with the affairs and the eventual divorce it really does not read as if these two should be held up as poster children for the value of romantic love, despite the exalted place they hold in the common consciousness. In all likelihood Napoleon was a little too busy conquering Europe and pestering the English to be that overwhelmingly concerned with his wife.

One of the most popular love stories of recent history is that of Edward Duke of Windsor and Wallis Simpson, or 'That American Woman' as she was generally known. Edward, the heir to the British throne, provoked national horror and a succession crisis when his father died. He refused to end his liaison with the once-divorced and twice-married Simpson when he ascended the throne as Edward VIII, risking the disapprobation of both Church and state. Despite her publicly stated willingness to give up their romance Edward was intractable, and on 10 December 1936 he abdicated in favour of his brother.

Ah, the sacrifices one makes for love. Like most such stories, though, it fades slightly when not viewed through rose-tinted glasses. Wallis and Edward were dogged with controversy about her alleged affairs and Nazi sympathising. When their love letters were eventually published after her death they stirred little interest other than some disappointment in their extreme banality. He burbles at her with babytalk and teenage rubbish, hardly the stuff of romantic legend: 'This is just to say good meesel and that I love you more and more before I make another drowsel', and 'a boy loves a girl more & more'. She, on the other hand, writes extremely practical missives that never stray into his soppy-floppy territory:

> Have the table moved back as far as possible and if the [Vansittarts] are coming there would be far more room for ten if the Finn could produce chairs without arms. Here is a suggestion for seating. I would also have two sorts of cocktails and white wine offered as well as the vin rosé, the servants to

> serve the wine. Also I didn't see a green vegetable on the menu. Sorry to bother you but I like everyone to think you do things well.[6]

There's little doubt that Wallis and Edward loved each other and that he made a huge sacrifice to be with her, but as an example of a heroic ardour to aspire to they fail miserably.

The chemical equation for love

For all the emphasis on romantic love in the West (and increasingly the rest of the world, weaned on a diet of Hollywood and reruns of *Friends*), the experience itself is neither as profound nor as sincere as we tend to assume. What we think of as a deep emotional connection or some inexplicable personal bond is usually just down to chemicals. Appearances to the contrary, this is not a cynical attack on the idea of love. People do unquestionably find each other and get carried away with grand passions that last a lifetime and are based in respect, caring and more than the irrational desire to screw someone silly until you both have orgasm-induced heart attacks. These people are *very lucky*. For the rest of us, however, it's worth remembering that what we take for a true romantic passion may be nothing more than our hormones playing games with us and trying to coerce us into breeding.

According to George Bernard Shaw, marriage brings people together 'under the influence of the most violent, most insane, most delusive and most transient of passions. They are required to swear that they will remain in that excited, abnormal and exhausting condition until death do them part'.[7] It's odd how willing we are to accept the dominance of our chemical make-up in the arena of love when we as a species spend so much time trying to fight off our baser instincts in other areas. Civilisation, we cry proudly: progress, modernity, movement. All these things are grand and respectable and desirable, leaving no room for animal passions or retrogressive desires; until, that is, we come to arena of love, when suddenly a transitory feeling becomes a worthy justification for all sorts of unreasonable behaviour.

Let's take a look at some of the common symptoms that surround falling in love. Sweaty palms? Racing heart? Feeling nervous, shaky, having trouble concentrating? Sounds less like a dream come true than like a bad case of flu. And it's not just physically that love resembles a disease – the chemical causes and effects are frighteningly close to the symptoms of substance abuse. Yup, that's right, drugs. Big, nasty, illegal drugs.

Dr John Marsden is a senior lecturer in Addictive Behaviour at London's Institute of Psychiatry and a senior member of the UK National Addiction Centre. He says that love is so addictive it's 'akin to cocaine and speed'.[8]

Nora Volkow, associated director for life sciences at Brookhaven National Laboratory in New York, analysed the behaviour of drug addicts and people in love, and found striking parallels. 'When a person is passionately in love it is extremely exciting and provocative, and if the loved one is not there, distressing,' she says. 'When I see my drug addicted patients it clicks how similar the addiction is.'[9]

Researchers Andreas Bartels and Semi Zeki conducted a study at University College London in 2000 using functional magnetic resonance imaging (fMRI) to monitor the brain activity of 17 subjects who described themselves as 'truly and madly' in love. The results were dramatic. When shown photographs of their lovers, the volunteers exhibited activity in four small areas of the brain – exactly the ones that have been shown to respond to euphoria-inducing drugs.[10]

Anthropologist Helen Fisher, a research professor at New Jersey's Rutgers University, knows more about it than most. In

2004 she published the critically lauded *Why We Love: The Nature and Chemistry of Romantic Love*, about the brain physiology of romantic attachment.[11] Fisher proposes that we fall in love in three stages, and that each stage is induced by different chemicals. Do any of these sound familiar?

The first stage, which she calls lust, is driven by testosterone and oestrogen, both found in both sexes in varying quantities. The lust impulse is fairly indiscriminate; it'll happily fasten onto an object who may be far from perfect in personal terms but exhibits attractive body language and speed and tone of voice. A study at the University of Chicago showed that the average man's testosterone levels jumped by an astonishing one-third during a casual chat with a female stranger, and his behaviour changed exponentially according to how much testosterone he produced.[12] Researchers suspect that this hormone jump may have something to do with the human male's 'mating response', as its levels are noticeably lower in married men and fathers than in single men. When you've sated the overwhelming physical urge to mate and procreate, your body calms you back down by producing a surge of hormones called endogenous opiates, which is a scientific name for the naturally occurring equivalent of heroin. Yup, it's those big scary drugs again.

Next comes attraction, the love-struck phase when people moon over each other in deeply romantic fashion, thinking about their lovers all day, becoming unnecessarily weepy, having trouble sleeping and forgetting to eat. This phase is regulated by a group of neurotransmitters called monoamines. These comprise dopamine (also found, not entirely surprisingly, in cocaine and nicotine), norepinephrine or adrenaline, which gets the heart racing, and serotonin, a lovely little chemical compound that can affect your mental health. An Italian study in 1990 found that people who were in love had up to 40 per cent less than the normal levels of serotonin, a similar amount to people suffering from severe obsessive compulsive disorder. (Been calling your lover a few times too many?)

A team from the University of Pisa, Italy, found that the body chemistry that makes people sexually attractive to new partners lasts a maximum of just two years – hardly a viable basis for making a life-long commitment.[13] The researchers tested volunteers' blood levels of the hormones called neutrophins. They found they were significantly higher in people in the early stages of romance but barely visible in the blood of people who'd been with their partners for one or two years, even if the relationships were stable. Team leader Donatella Marazziti said, 'If lovers swear their feelings to be ever-lasting, the hormones tell a different story.' Similar research conducted by Enzo Emanuele at the University of Pavia found that levels of a chemical messenger called nerve growth factor (NGF) increased with romantic intensity but went back to normal levels after one or two years.[14] We have to wonder why the Italians are doing so much research into the biology of love; perhaps they're more plagued with it than most.

Fisher's third stage is attachment, which keeps couples together for longer, particularly when they have children. This is regulated by hormones that seem to play an important role in socialising us. Oxytocin, known as the 'cuddling chemical', is released by the hypothalamus of both partners during orgasm and by the woman's during childbirth. It helps new mothers express milk, allowing for bonding between parent and child, and promotes pair bonding between adults, which should help them stay together until their child is old enough to survive physically without two parents.

Another hormone, vasopressin, was isolated after experiments with frisky prairie voles, one of the rare examples in the natural world of animals having sex far more than they need to for procreation. They're randy little buggers but they also mate for the long term. After they sex each other up, the voles release both of these hormones. In an experiment male voles were given vasopressin-suppressing drugs. The bonds with their partners vanished almost immediately, they lost their devotion and failed to protect their former loved ones from the attention of new suitors.

In addition, these chemical processes are not tied to each other chronologically and can operate independently. It's perfectly possible to feel a deep overwhelming first-stage desire for a new person while still maintaining your third-stage attachment to your child's other parent.

Humans are not, however, prairie voles. We're more complex and more self-aware, at least in ideal conditions. Surely, then, knowledge of these chemical inconsistencies needs to be tempered by acknowledging our finer feelings and emotional/intellectual intricacy? Indeed. And no one is claiming that love doesn't exist, that it's a myth or only down to the biological urge to reproduce. Let's not make the mistake of thinking that just because there are chemical triggers for the feeling of love that love itself is a chimera, an opiate for the masses drawn up by some shady latter-day conspiracy to keep us all busy so we don't notice them using CIA-trained marine animals to take over the world.

That said, unless you're insanely lucky, insanely foolish, a teenager or a poet, chances are you won't fall madly in love that many times in your life, and your desires for other people will usually stop at the lust phase. Which means that every time it hits you it'll be new and overwhelming. Rather than having a chance to get accustomed to the effects of these love drugs and to figure out where your real emotions lie, you'll be swept away in a raging torrent of hormonal desire. You'll believe that you've never been more right or felt anything more real, despite the uncharacteristic way you're behaving and your lover's qualities that would annoy or appal you in anyone else.

This is not the wisest state to be in when making a decision as huge as committing to spending your life with another person. It's equivalent to a woman who suffers from horrible PMT signing a mortgage agreement three days before her period when she's ever so slightly insane. The difference is, of course, that she's had years to get used to the effects of her hormones so she knows that they come and go, and that she just needs to wait them out and get some perspective on the situation. If there's one thing lovers are short of, it's perspective.

'The main conclusion I've reached is that love, or least romantic love, is not an emotion,' Fisher explains.

> The emotion centres in the brain become active when we're in love, true, but in actual fact it's a drive. It utilises the same centres as focussed, active, goal-oriented behaviour. All drives hook into the dopamine system. Romantic love just doesn't have the characteristics of an emotion. Think about it. When someone's angry you can see it on their face – that's emotion. But when someone's hungry you can't tell just by looking at them; hunger's a drive, and love is like hunger. You cannot tell from someone's expressions whether they're in love or not.
>
> Romantic love is actually far, far stronger than the sex drive. If you ask someone whether they want to go to bed with you and they say no, chances are you won't try to kill yourself. We get sexually rejected all the time without reacting in the extreme way we do when we get rejected in love. Love can drive people to suicide, to killing someone else, to stalking them, all sorts of irrational behaviour; sex doesn't do that. Not only is romantic love a drive, it's a very powerful one – sometimes it can be stronger than the will to live itself. It's a profoundly basic drive, too, fundamental to all spheres of

human behaviour – just look at all the poetry, lyrics, music, art it's inspired over the history of civilisation.

The drive to attach can sometimes be stronger than the love drive though – sometimes people will stay in mediocre marriages instead of running off with the objects of their love because they're already attached. But in other cases romantic love overrides it or the pure sex drive takes over and someone will leave a fairly happy marriage quite easily. It's hard to tell what makes these situations what they are, but once we're attached there may be children or personal comfort involved and it becomes cognitive, a question of psychology interacting with these drives. It's all about the ratios between these systems and other systems.[15]

So go ahead – have your glorious romance. Hell, have three. Have as many as you can possibly get. But don't go fixating on some romantic ideal of love as a good reason to make a concrete life decision, not unless you've thought about it very, very carefully. There may not have been studies done on what happens to couples who're locked together when the hormone rush fades, but now that divorce is a viable option for most Westerners, the statistics are probably a clue to that figure. It's akin to waking up with a hangover and that pesky new tattoo.

Two case studies

Georgina, 30 and English, had been in four serious relationships before she met her husband Wens, and was engaged to three of her exes. 'I'd never really believed in marriage despite being engaged so often,' she says. 'When I finally decided to get married, it seemed right with Wens because I genuinely wanted to spend the rest of my life with him. He's from the Congo, so there was also the thing of us saving money on renewing his student visa and him eventually getting leave to remain in the UK. We were living apart at the time and he never in the eight-month marriage moved from London to be with me. I know now that I was used for his visa, and for money too, but at the time I loved him; I couldn't see him for what he was.'

It wasn't a case of social pressure. She'd been with Wens for seven months when he proposed. 'My family didn't approve and my friends were supportive despite thinking I was making a grave mistake. I'm a headstrong person and tend to do what I want anyway, so no matter what anyone said I would have gone through with it.

'At my hen party I started to worry about what I was doing and wish I was having a normal wedding. My father called me to make sure I still wanted to go through with it. I did but I had some serious doubts, which I ignored.

'The whole thing cost less than £500, licences included. I did my own hair and make-up and we didn't have flowers to save money. I wore a trouser suit that I really hate now, it wasn't me at all. My parents came but they looked like they were going to a funeral. There wasn't a reception, we just went to the pub. I hardly saw my husband all night because he was enjoying himself with his friends, and we had an argument because he refused to dance with me but danced very sexily with another woman. I spent most of the night with my best friend.

'I knew in my heart that something was wrong as life between us just went back to normal, him in London, me in Dover. We were nothing like how I thought husband and wife should be. His friends were nicer to me than he was at times. He started to go out more without me, expecting me to be happy with not seeing him for three weeks at a time. He also wouldn't have sex with me as he claimed he was ill. He expected me to behave like a stereotypical "good African wife", to tolerate his ways, let him go out all the time with his friends and just produce babies.

'The marriage eventually ended after I found out that he cheated on me – and I doubt it was the only time. I found a text message on his phone. I called the girl, who admitted to fucking him and insisted she knew nothing about me. He denied everything. A few days later, by accident, I overheard a whole 90 minutes of him chatting up some girl and asking her to be his girlfriend. It was like having my heart ripped out all over again. He begged to be allowed come back, crying on his knees in public (oh, the power I felt!), but after two months I finally decided enough was enough.

'The divorce has been relatively easy. With each step I felt like a weight has been lifted. I'm waiting for the decree nisi at the moment, and when that comes through I'll be like a new woman.

'My family are really relieved. No one said I told you so. My father's even come to see me at 2 am sometimes when I'd had an emotional breakdown. My friends were wonderful, and my best mate came with me to collect the few things I had at his house – she was my getaway driver! Everyone I've met since has been very supportive and loving. I have never been judged, despite being the fool for being taken in by him.'

So would she consider getting married again? 'No, I now know in my heart that I don't need a piece of paper to prove someone loves me.'

Georgina's marriage was a nightmare, a car crash that she could not predict. When they say love is blind this is precisely what they mean. True, she's past the worst of it now and has her life back, but think of her as a cautionary tale for all those moments when your love feels so strong that you just *know* what you're doing is right.

Sophie is 26, bright, beautiful and frighteningly articulate. She's been with her boyfriend for a couple of years now and they're pretty serious. They're both private people who like their space, and each currently chooses to live alone, but he's considering giving up his Berlin flat, good job and close friends to move to the United States when she goes there to study later this year. Despite the massive upheaval and commitment the move would entail, they're not even considering marriage. Why should they, when everything's working so well?

She explains, 'For me, marriage has never been part of my dreams for the future. It has never entered my mind as a concept to be longed for, missed, or something to work toward. Even though my parents have been married for 40-odd years and clearly couldn't live without one another I still don't see "marriage" as the miracle. For me, it is more about actually living together, making it work, wanting to be together so much that you stay together for years. It is even more amazing if you have kids and make it work. If this life that two people share is happy, it is of no consequence if they are married or not.

'I was never a staunch feminist who rejected "patriarchal structures of oppression" and thought marriage subordinated women. I was a real 1980s' kid with loads of Barbie dolls and other not so politically correct gender-forming toys, and I remember hearing tales of princes and princesses and big white dresses and happy forever after. But all that left me completely indifferent to marriage. And "indifferent" is the word – I neither love nor hate the idea. I just fail to see the point of it (beyond the clear economic privileges and security for your children that come with marriage in certain countries – a fact that clearly discriminates against people who choose not to get married). It has gone so far that when attending weddings, I am not particularly moved by two people promising to live together for the rest of their lives. I kind of want to say, "Well just do it, then!" Because saying it is one thing, doing it is a whole other bag of chips. Maybe I am disillusioned with the whole vow thing because I know that half of all marriages end in divorce. I don't know.

'I cannot see that my partner and I have lost anything by not getting married. It has never been a subject of conversation between us. I think marriage is still, for many people at least, a very important institution of private/public life. I have the impression that all people who decide to marry do it for different reasons but that "marriage" is still a strong umbrella term that somehow ties all the different marriages together. For me, bizarrely enough (since my parents are still happily together and I have no close friends who have been divorced), I think the connotations go something like "boring, predictable, have to do such-and-such things and avoid such-and-such things". Being a "wife" will replace being "me"; being publicly and privately defined by an inherently conservative institution sucks.

'And where did the romance go? I have no idea. I guess I can't see how an institution like marriage should have a monopoly on defining romance or love or closeness or intimacy. That's something that happens to people regardless of documents and rituals.

'I honestly don't know what would change if I were married. I think I might suddenly feel sucked into this construction. I guess some of it has to do with my still wanting to keep my freedom to be "just me". I would like to keep the feeling for just a bit longer.'

So there you have it. Marrying for love or not marrying, precisely, for love. The trick is in knowing how to recognise your own emotional truth, behind the hormones, the chemicals, the drama, the expectations, the love songs, the fairytales. You may want to bone them all day now, but is this really the person you want to be helping you into your walking frame? Will you still find your partner appealing when your sexual urges are a distant memory and he or she smells of wee? Are you *that* much in love?

Chapter Two

'We did it for the benefits'

Chapter One may have come down quite harshly on the naïve tendency to get married for woolly romantic reasons that fade like sweet memories in the hard light of day, but at least those who wed for a bleary-eyed concept of love believe that there's something in their relationship worth cementing. (Either that or they've watched too many movies.) Possibly in more trouble, and even more deluded, are the category who marry their partners for passports, or tax breaks, or health insurance, for they radically underestimate the social power of the institution of marriage, assuming they can use it for their own purposes with no ill effects.

You might be able to write marriage off as 'just a piece of paper', and well done to you if you can, but you're ignoring all the consequences and the generations of connotation that this particular piece of paper comes burdened with. No matter what we as individuals think marriage is, no matter how lightly we're capable of taking it or how clearly we can see what it means to us, it is a heavily weighted social construction that has oceans of significance for our society, our culture and the people around us. It would be foolish to pretend that none of that has an effect on how we feel and respond, or on what the eventual corollaries of a marriage will be.

More than once while researching this book I encountered people who told me how surprised they'd been when their fun, friendly lover, who seemed to share their opinion on the subject completely, did the last thing they were expecting and suddenly turned into the sort of person to whom marriage is no laughing matter. If you truly believe you can get married and appreciate what it will add to your life without risking any less pleasing consequences, then you're either living in a dream world or marrying a saint. Like the old adage says, you don't get nothing for nothing; and even if you're paying your prospective spouse a couple of thousand to do it, there may still be lurking costs that neither of you has considered.

Immigration and 'fake' marriages

People get married for passports all the time. Border controls, immigration problems, endemic poverty and persistent social and economic injustice dictate that there will always be people wealthy, brave or desperate enough to do whatever it takes to make a better life for themselves. Most of the time this better life involves migration to a country with healthcare, or social welfare, or education, or even just the very basic right to walk around your home town without dodging bullets or running from rapists. It's easy for us in the first world to underestimate the terror faced by people who live in war zones or extreme poverty. Our right-wing press consistently laments the loose borders and laws that allow immigrants in, but we hear considerably less about the conditions they come from and about our direct or indirect responsibility for their situation. It's worth thinking about our governments selling arms to countries with worrying human rights records, or propping up unequal systems of trade that make imports from the first world cheaper than local produce, destroying third world agriculture.

In the UK, rightist tabloids are quick to stir up panic with their provocative headlines[1] but are a lot less sharp on the uptake when it comes to reporting the real facts about the country's intake of refugees. Contrary to the invasion horror stories trumpeted by the press, the United Kingdom has only 21,000 refugees and asylum seekers; compare this with Sweden's 23,900, Canada's 43,300, France's 46,400 and South Africa's 171,300.[2] Nor do they often mention how many of those who arrive here have been tortured and threatened with death by their own governments. We're all so hung up on the idea of immigrants spongeing off us that we can't see the wood for the trees.

Vigilante groups in the United States will happily patrol the Texan border looking for Mexicans who try to sneak under the radar. Incidences of shootings and even murder sometimes involving the US Border Patrol are commonplace. In August 2001 the Mexican government condemned a court in Eagle Pass, Texas, that found 74-year-old Samuel Blackwood guilty of homicide in the death of 22-year-old Mexican border jumper Eusebio de Haro – and sentenced him to a shockingly minimal six months imprisonment. These angry US citizens spend a lot less time being concerned about the teenage girls who have been forced into prostitution by economic privation in Tijuana, which mainly serves US college students on party breaks. Since Denver passed the country's toughest law against illegal immigration in 2006, there's been such a labour shortage that farms are having to employ convicts. So no, it is not within the remit of this book to criticise those who will utilise any means necessary to get out of their country of origin. The level of desperation evinced by many of the world's refugees far outweighs considerations of fakery.

That said, though, many of those who get married for visa reasons are nowhere near this kind of anguish. They're often economic migrants, educated and with earning power, who choose to move to new countries. And all too often this class of people sees marriage as nothing but a convenient way to circumvent the system. Which it can be, no question, but it's likely to be a whole lot more as well.

Now I'm not pleading the sanctity of the bond between man and wife, which would be just a little hypocritical considering the nature of this book. What I am doing is pointing out to the self-deluding that marriage is a legal and social contract, and no matter how hard you try to pretend otherwise, it has ramifications that you may not be anticipating. Even if you're completely clear-headed about what your marriage means and does not mean, others may not be so sensible.

Daniel is South African, from a conservative city in the Cape. He left for England after university, aged just 21, on a working holiday visa, planning to make some money and then head back home to start his 'real' life. But after two years he had fallen in love with the pace and excitement of London and desperately wanted to stay. Daniel is gay, and for the first time in his life he'd found acceptance and a world he felt he belonged in.

He says, 'After I'd been in London for a while, I realised there was no way I could just go back to Stellenbosch. My parents didn't know I was gay and there was no gay scene at my university even though it's so close to Cape Town. It wasn't about the clubs or the nightlife even, it was about having a community for the first time. So I was really, really happy when one of my friends offered to marry me. We're in the same crowd, we're still good friends now, and she's gay too so it wasn't a problem for her to do it. It wasn't like she would be wanting to get married. I didn't tell my parents, they have no idea how stuff works in the UK so I just let them assume I worked something out with my visa. They were a bit confused that I didn't want to come home, but I was making good money and I had an interesting job so they let it go.'

Picture perfect, isn't it? Except things didn't work out that easily.

'The ceremony itself was very casual,' he continues. 'We had two friends as witnesses, one of them from back home, and I thought they were both quite understanding of the whole situation. Turns out that one was but the other wasn't. He went back home about a year later, and suddenly he was telling all his friends what he'd been up to and saying things like, "Oh yeah, I was a witness at Daniel's wedding. Daniel's married." I think that even though he knew it was for a passport, he kind of assumed a wedding's a wedding.

'So I started getting emails from people going, "I heard you got married, congratulations." And then of course the news spread because it's quite a small town, and someone congratulated my mom. Which was terrible because she had no idea, so I had her on the phone in tears thinking I'd married some stranger and not invited her. She was really heartbroken. The end result was that I had to come out [as gay] to my parents over the phone from another continent, which is really not how you want to do it. I don't know what was worse for them, me not telling them I was married or me being a *moffie*.[3]

'It's fine now, they're my parents and they love me. But I'm still really angry with the so-called friend who blabbed it all over town. Every time someone asks my mom when I'll start having kids or when I'll bring my wife home she has to smile and nod. It's too hard for her to tell people I'm gay, especially when I'm not around to make it seem less freaky. My father just grunts at questions, no one asks him anything anyway. It's not a complete disaster, and of course I got to stay in London where I'm now very settled. But I still wish to God that that stupid guy hadn't talked about it. I don't think he knows how much heartache he caused.'

And then, of course, there is the tiny matter that sham marriages are deeply illegal.[4] It is illegal for anyone to get married solely for the purpose of getting, or helping someone else to get, permanent residence in the United States. US law is fairly self-explanatory when it comes to penalties for wannabe immigrants attempting to con their way in: 'Any individual who knowingly enters into a marriage for the purpose of evading any provision of the immigration laws shall be imprisoned for not more than five years, or fined not more than $250,000, or both.' Harsh punishment indeed – and of course the applicant will also be refused entry into the promised land for the rest of his or her life. The US citizen or resident, meanwhile, could also face criminal prosecution, including fines or imprisonment. In some cases a legal US resident may have their residency revoked and be deported back to their country of origin.

Officers of the US Citizenship and Immigration Services (USCIS) take immigration fraud extremely seriously. A survey from the 1980s claimed that 30 per cent of marriages between US citizens and foreigners were fakes; it's since been proved to be an enormous exaggeration, but its legacy of suspicion lives on.[5] And in our post-9/11 world, immigration has become even more of a political hot potato. You might think that you look harmless but to an over-enthusiastic USCIS man you could well be the personification of all evil, another shifty foreigner with questionable associations trying to scam your way into the land of the free.

It's not just the United States that's inundated with suspect marriage requests. In 2004–5 the Australian Immigration Department received 1,909 allegations of contrived marriages and relationships, a rise of 22.4 per cent on the previous year.[6] And as the statistics increase, so do the penalties. A 2005 report from the country's Department of Immigration and Multicultural and Indigenous Affairs stated (DIMIA), 'Organised contrived marriages and relationships are a high priority for DIMIA investigation activity and persons convicted can face penalties of up to ten years imprisonment and a fine of up to $100,000.'

Fake marriage is endemic in the United Kingdom too. Registrars at Brent Council in north London, one of the country's most ethnically diverse areas, suggested in 2005 that a fifth of all marriages booked there were bogus, with officials even spotting couples who obviously barely knew each other attempting to get married. Until recent legislation cracked down on fake marriages, registrars suggested there could have been at least 10,000 attempts a year. While there's no set punishment for sham marriages, the penalties can include fines, imprisonment, denial of citizenship and dissolution of the marriage.

The UK's Immigration and Naturalisation Department recently introduced a Certificate of Approval (COA) that an unmarried alien has to apply for before he or she can wed in the United Kingdom. One of the conditions is having more than three months left on a valid UK visa. Since the maximum allowance for a tourist visa is three months, it's bye-bye to coming over from your home country in order to get married – you have to establish a right to be in the United Kingdom before you can even think about finding a way to stay there. Some human rights groups have condemned this legislation, saying it discriminates against legitimate couples who may not be permanently resident and wish to marry, but whether they're morally kosher or not, the COA rules are now set.

New Zealand meanwhile declined 122 applications for residency based on marriage in 2006, a total of about 5 per cent.[7] As well as these denials, about half a dozen cases are prosecuted every year, which doesn't count the much larger majority who are rumbled in the application process and never get far enough for prosecution. While it's not illegal to exchange money for marriage there, it is an offence to provide misleading information to immigration officers. This includes saying you've been together for longer than you have, saying you're a couple when you're not and claiming you live together when you don't.

If officers aren't satisfied that the marriage is genuine and the relationship has been stable for a certain period of time they won't grant residence to the foreign partner. Applications can also be denied on the basis of health or character requirements, so anyone too dodgy will be weeded out, married or not. If you get far enough to be granted residency and then get busted for a fake marriage, the penalty is seven years imprisonment and/or a whopping great fine of up to NZ$100,000.

According to officials, most fake marriages that make it to prosecution are uncovered after calls and letters from members of the public. Add to this immigration officials' own detective work and the prospect starts to look a little less appealing.

Many people are not deterred by the threat of punishment, however, assuming that it'll be easy to get away with. Surely all you have to do is just get married? But no, there tends to be a little more to it. Most countries have similar rules requiring you to prove the validity of your relationship over a period of time. If you get married in the country you want to live in you'll usually be granted conditional residence for a few years, after which you'll have to prove that you're still with your spouse. But a lot can happen in that time.

What if you marry your lover but it all goes horribly wrong and you break up within a year? Will you still be able to depend on that person to see the process through with you? What if the break-up is really bad and they don't want anything to do with you? What if they meet someone else they want to marry? What if one of you has a child with someone else? All these variables will count when you peek your head around the immigration services' door two years later, begging to be granted the elusive gold of permanent resident status. Pinning all your hopes on someone else, even if you do manage to avoid the legal penalties and consequences, can still leave you deeply in the lurch when crunch time comes.

If you marry someone for a passport, apply for temporary residence but then no longer have the support of your spouse when the requisite time period is up, you'll be worse off than you were before. The immigration service now has a record of you, so any other attempt you make to stay in the country will look extremely suspicious. Getting married for a passport is just not the most sensible or safe method of immigration. (Still, it beats the hell out of clinging to the bottom of a Channel-going truck.)

Kagai is in his early 30s. Originally from Kenya, he's been living in the United Kingdom for close on ten years, most of those illegally after his attempt at marrying someone for a passport went horribly wrong. He's also found himself a wonderful woman he'd love to marry, but it's not easy now that he's on the government's radar.

He explains, 'Me and Justine had been together for one year and then we decided to get married. We were just two crazy kids. She decided to marry me probably because I'm a good shag, I don't know, I don't know what her reasons were.

'We were together for three years I think, but we started arguing very quickly. We used to party a lot, do cocaine. She was going a bit crazy from the drugs. She did too much. She was doing it at work even, lines in toilets on Tuesday or Wednesday in the day. We argued a lot about that. We also started fighting about papers. There were things she was supposed to sign but she didn't.

'She married me to help me but she also liked me. That was the deal, but she broke the deal. She freaked out too much, went crazy, and she fucked me up with her.

'We were supposed to go to the Home Office but we had a big argument so she didn't turn up, which meant I was really screwed. My lawyer was there, going "Where is your wife?" Everyone was going "Where is your wife?" I tried to explain, but they said I had to book another appointment. And I tried to do that but she wouldn't come with me because she was too angry, so eventually they went, "Well, this is not a real marriage."

'Luckily for me, because of the way the laws were then, they couldn't kick me directly out of the country because I was still married, otherwise I would have been in real trouble. They took away my National Insurance card and tried to stop me working, so eventually I ended up disappearing, going underground. That was it for us as far as I was concerned because she really didn't stick to her side of the deal.

'She went to Brazil and when she came back she was three months pregnant and thought I was going to be with her. I was already with my fiancée Kathy then, and anyway I wasn't interested. Me and Justine, we didn't know each other when we got married and there were too many drugs involved.

'Recently I went to a solicitor about getting divorced and marrying Kathy. The Home Office said I would have to go back to Kenya and marry her there and they would give me a piece of paper that said I could come back. The solicitor tried to get the paper out of them but they kept refusing and I don't believe they're going to do it.

'I don't know what me and Kathy are going to do now but we're going to have to think of a plan because I'm stuck in England but we can't get married in England. If I leave I can never come back.'

And then, of course, there are certain risks for the person who's a resident in the chosen country. Witness again Georgina's story, related in Chapter One, of how she was persuaded to marry a man who not only did not love her but, once the wedding was over, couldn't be bothered to show the courtesy of pretending to love her.

Hollywood hysteria

Many people of my generation will have seen the 1990 movie *Green Card*, a piece of unapologetic romantic twaddle in which Andie MacDowell's bloodless gardener is so desperate to acquire a couples-only apartment that she engages in a fake marriage with Gerard Depardieu, an impressively beaked Frenchman who will go to all sorts of lengths to get his Gallic hands on the eponymous green card. Quite apart from MacDowell's scandalous lack of passion (and indeed personality) and her beau's completely impenetrable accent, the film's major crime against taste, decency and the American way is to have these two chalk-and-cheese types fall deeply in love once they're married. (That's after the requisite initial hatred, without which Hollywood romcoms would be nothing but Barbara Cartland with different accents.) Cruel immigration officials attempt to part them, cultural differences threaten the purity of their devotion, but finally love conquers all and our intercontinental sweethearts end up living happily ever after in a great big Hallmark card of eye-gazing hand-holding teeth-baring inanity.

This film has much to answer for, mainly in the arena of why on earth anyone would think the world needs yet another vapid *vive la difference* excuse for a love story. (That said, in today's climate of psycho invasion jocks and cheese-eating surrender monkeys the United States and France could probably use a good healthy dose of *amour*.) But more than that, it is also responsible for the gross romanticisation of the dangerous, dodgy and downright depressing passport marriage. Mention such a situation to a woman of my age and chances are she'll glaze over, sigh deeply and say, 'Oh, just like in *Green Card*. Wow, I bet you'll fall in love with each other,' which is what we've all been unconsciously trained to do by the subliminal messages implanted in decades worth of brain-numbing blockbusters. The reality, dear readers, tends to be either far more prosaic or far more unpleasant.

Like Daniel, Nicholas got married so he could stay in England. Unlike Daniel, however, part of his reason was to be with his British girlfriend. And though she willingly married him the eventual consequences for their relationship were dire.

'I'd been going out with Chloe for a year and a half when we got married,' he says. 'My visa was expiring soon and I was all set to go back to New Zealand. She offered to marry me really casually: "Well, let's get married and then you can stay," because at that point we were seriously into each other. Neither of us knew where our relationship was going but we knew we didn't want to break up, so it was the obvious solution.'

He explains, 'I was very clear in my mind about the separation between a legal marriage and a relationship commitment, and I thought she was too, but I wasn't mature enough to discuss it fully with her, and now I realise that I never really knew how she felt. She was doing it partly as a favour to me and partly because she liked me.

'Getting married didn't really change anything about how we lived. I was very defensive with my friends about the fact that I wasn't actually married, which I suppose Chloe could have seen as a slight rejection because I was always saying, "No no, it's just a legal marriage." Afterwards we never talked seriously about future plans; it was always fantasies, let's go there or live in that exotic place. Quite a bit later when things got rocky both of us became aware that there was this silence when it came to talking about our futures. I was much more silent than she was, I think talking about future plans would have made me acknowledge that I didn't want to be with her. And part of that fear was the fear of our marriage, because we were married but we *weren't* married, and suddenly I found that we were in a really strange place. Being married made it a vastly more thorny situation.

'The first time we broke up I know she definitely wanted to be with me although by then I couldn't really conceive of being with her, but of course I had to stay with her because we were married. Even then I refused to acknowledge the effect that the visa thing had on our relationship, but now I see that it was very important because it put us into this weird limbo. It wasn't a reason to stay together but it certainly complicated things a lot. Visa and marriage aside, I would have broken up with her a lot sooner.

'When things were really bad we started talking about where we were going. And of course the future, when people have been together for four, five years, is marriage. I was thinking, how can we get married even though we are married? What would that mean? Would I now see her as my wife when she'd been my "married girlfriend"? We'd done the symbolic thing but it had no substance for us. I think the symbolism of marriage affects you if you're partners, you can't get away from it because every relationship has to grow and develop. If you're together and you want to stay together you do something to mark it. But if you're unsure of that or forced into it, it's very confusing.

'I didn't want to move to where she wanted to go, so the only thing to do was to get out. There wasn't another way to rejig it, partly because we were married. The moral of the story is that getting married has significant implications for relationships where marriage could be an issue at some point.

It's not just a legal thing, despite what we thought. Initially Chloe was very irreverent towards the whole idea of marriage, partly because she was in an irreverent stage of her life: you know, young, free, rebellious. But I think she didn't realise that irreverence was only skin deep.

'The end result of the marriage was huge amounts of bitterness from Chloe towards me. I've got no contact with her now, which is quite a shame. A lot of time, a lot of memories; we grew up together. I see it as very much a distant part of my history. I'm starting to change my story in a sense – instead of a "we" it's now a "me" when I talk about that part of my life. And I know she's doing the same. We've written each other out.'

Marriage and the money myth

Of course that's just one couple's story of how marriage eroded their relationship. Surely, I hear you say, the benefits outweigh the risks? What about all those tax breaks I keep hearing about? Like many of the myths surrounding marriage there is both truth and absence of truth in these claims.

In the United States, the 'marriage penalty' has recently been repealed. This was a tax that couples accrued when they filed joint taxes, usually costing around $1,300. Despite this hefty sum the penalty was something of a red herring as these same couples generally recouped their losses in tax breaks. It may have looked like a good situation for newlyweds but upon closer examination there were some serious disparities. The couples that got the most tax breaks were those with a vast gap between partners' incomes, while couples who earned similar amounts tended to face a bigger marriage penalty.

There's really no point beating around the bush here – the unarguable fact is that in the large majority of couples with disparate incomes, the husband earns more than the wife. So if the hubby made loads and the wife had some cutesy little job on the side, they got tax benefits. If, however, they both earned similar amounts, which meant the missus also had a Real Job, they got fewer breaks. So who was penalised here? Working women. Yep, there may have been some financial advantages to marriage, but they didn't do much for gender equality. Now this penalty has been removed, of course, it's no longer an issue; but let's just wait and see what else Congress comes up with to ensure complicity in the great scheme of 'keeping everyone quietly married and breeding so they don't get in the way of our wars', also known as the Family Values Agenda. This is one of the secret motivations behind marriage benefits: they're not just about you being married, they're about *how your marriage works*. Stay-at-home wives seem, as a rule, to do better than working women when it comes to getting marital benefits from the state.

Despite the commonly held belief that it gives married people a better deal, the United Kingdom has a system of independent taxation of husbands and wives for income tax and capital gains tax that removes many of the benefits of being married. Sure, there are *some* advantages. Spouses can transfer capital gains between themselves without being taxed, which can allow the one who earns less to claim the other's money on his or her non-taxable allowance. Inheritance tax, too, does not apply to spouses: you can leave your entire estate to your husband or wife without incurring tax – a situation which inspires much-deserved wrath in long-term couples who prefer not to get married and are penalised for daring to break with the conventional order.

Even these advantages are not much to write home about, and certainly not enough to base a marriage on. Chas Roy-Chowdhury, head of taxation at the Association of Chartered Certified Accountants, says, 'If you are thinking of getting married do it for love, not for any tax benefit – you would have to really scratch your head to try and find any big tax advantages to being married.'

One of the most startling facts in this area is that tax breaks for married people, like most tax breaks, are more beneficial the more money you have. Yes, even though these economic benefits are not as striking as they have been in the past, it's another case of the rich getting richer and the poor getting poorer. Social Security taxes in the United States still routinely penalise working spouses – again, mainly women.

According to the Social Security Administration, the body that deals with the country's welfare system, around 62 per cent of widowed women over the age of 62 who claim benefits do so on the basis of their late husbands' financial contribution rather than their own, which is a right all citizens have. Some of these women never earned enough to qualify for Social Security at all; many opted to take their husbands' cheques as they were bigger. In one sense marriage is advantageous for them – they get more money because they can claim the Social Security of their higher-earning husbands. But in another it's a great big cheat. These women receive *absolutely nothing* from their own Social Security contributions over the years. They might as well have never paid a cent for all the benefits they get; they'd be in the same position of sitting on their husbands' incomes if they had never bothered to work. The state pays out for the higher-earning partner only and gets to hold onto whatever the lower earner paid in over the years.

Social Security taxes take 6.2 per cent of every US worker's pay cheque, and employers contribute an equal amount. All of this money, painstakingly paid out by low-income working women, is ignored when they choose their husbands' Social Security benefits. Where does it go, these years of payments that should have been returned to them? To funding better education in deprived inner-city areas, improved health care, infrastructure, disaster relief for poor communities like those devastated by Hurricane Katrina? Or possibly the purchase of more weapons or the building of more prison camps away from the beady eyes of US human rights lawyers?

As the Hurricane Katrina fiasco revealed in black and white, there's not a huge amount of money being earmarked for the poor in the United States, and it's clear that the Social Security contributions of low-income women, never returned to them directly, are also not being invested in their communities. Not only is this drastically unfair on so many levels, it also disincentivises women to work. That's a consequence that seems to be painfully common, as we saw above, especially considering the demonisation of working mothers that occurs in much of the Western press.

Staying away from marriage is statistically more beneficial for women's pockets anyway, no matter how much men may bemoan the existence of alimony payments. A total 14.9 per cent of all married women in the United States earned at least $5,000 more than their partners in 1997; for unmarried women that figure rose to 21.5 per cent. The male partner was the only one employed in 22.4 per cent of marriages, compared with 18.2 per cent in unmarried couples. The female partner was the only one with a job in just 6.8 per cent of married couples, rising to 10.7 per cent in unmarried couples. Both partners were in employment in 53.5 per cent of married couples against 65 per cent of unmarried couples. It seems that, however things work out for a couple, financial independence for women thrives best outside marriage, as does the ability to have a career and the self-determination that brings.

Perhaps marriage can benefit you slightly when it comes to the end of the financial year – but should it? How ethically correct is this, that your two-partner home should be handed advantages denied to a single person who works just as hard because your government wants to bribe the populace into a demographic it feels more comfortable with? We already spend an inordinate amount of time being told what to eat, how much to exercise, how to look after ourselves, how to behave. UK commentators have had a field day in the past few years denouncing Tony Blair's 'nanny state' and its obsessive desire to regulate every aspect of its patients' – sorry, citizens' – lives.

Financial incentives for marriage, minimal though they may be, are yet another way for our leaders to run our personal affairs. The idealised conception of mum and dad and Billy and Sue as 'The Family' that is so often spouted by (affair-having prostitute-frequenting secretly homosexual) politicians is a Victorian invention. It's tied to the adoption of love as a reason to wed, and the shift from extended in-law-based families to the nuclear model. Marriage may indeed have been one of the building blocks of civilisation, but that was a very different kind of marriage. The partnership that governments are pushing now is an emotional, love-based affair, idyllic and impractical, not at all the sociocultural glue it's implied to be. And this is what they're paying us to do? Rather than adapt to a changing environment our leaders are trying to cement the 'old' order of things, an order that's clearly on its way out and was never that widespread anyway, by offering us money. These tactics would work on truculent teenagers but they shouldn't have any effect on grown-ups.

In the United Kingdom it's not just Tony Blair who's trying to tell his children – sorry, electorate – how to live. The leader of the Conservative Party, David 'Dave' Cameron, has suggested reintroducing tax benefits for the married in a shocking turn of events that's actually forced this humble author to agree with Blair.[8] Cameron, campaigning on the basis of his respect for The Family, supported the reintroduction of tax breaks for married people at the expense of those antisocial ASBO-courting loonies who choose not to get married.[9] In March 2007 he said:

> This is not about saying single parents do a bad job. They do the hardest job in the world. It is simply saying that kids do best when mum and dad are both there for them. That's why we support marriage. Some people say it's wrong to single out marriage in this way. I don't care.[10]

Well, Dave, as cheering as it is to hear you utter such a brave 'punk-style' fuck 'em all statement, divorce and single-parent families have been on the increase for years. You are not going to turn the tide of this social trend by offering people a few quid a year to get married; what you are going to do is penalise the children of unmarried parents. Sure, doubtless most kids are happier with mum and dad together, but some extra cash to supplement mum's shoddy income from the only crap job that lets her work part-time so she can be at home in the afternoons would also help. Annoyingly, Blair said it best:

> It's hard to see why you would want to support a married couple without children rather than a lone parent whose husband may have left her through no fault of her own and who is trying to bring up two children. Of course we should try to support marriage in whatever way we can, but to reduce support for lone parents isn't justified.[11]

The fact is that very few people who were definitely not intending to get married are likely to change their life plans completely just because someone offers them a tax break. Long-term couples may be swayed, yes, but those who choose to remain single or be lone parents are not going to alter their entire existence because someone offers them a little present. In effect all this is doing is rewarding people who behave in a way that Cameron thinks is 'right' and punishing those who do 'wrong'.

I have a few female friends who are single mothers, some of more than one child. I also have some male friends who don't live with their kids but do their level best to be involved fathers under these strained circumstances. As a rule, all struggle financially but manage to bring their kids up with love, respect, education, tolerance, wisdom, humour and an impressively small amount of junk food and bad TV. Some of the women have feckless exes who couldn't handle the pressure, some broke up due to relationship crises, some got pregnant unexpectedly and decided to have their babies anyway, some were single and running out of time.[12] Some of the men got a girlfriend pregnant by mistake, some had a bad relationship that had no hope of working out, some were involved with the wrong woman, some are better fathers than their exes are mothers but are still pushed to the sidelines by the social assumption that women make more effective parents. But they're all doing their best to make it work.[13] These people are tough and brave and they deserve as much support as they can get. It is not the government's job to give us cakes for being good children.

The downsides of marriage

Meanwhile, alongside the many not so very apparent 'advantages' of marriage come a host of disadvantages. I don't mean just the things you lose by being part of a couple, like the freedom to give that hunky barman the eye, refuse to shave your legs for six months or move to Italy on a whim and learn to make pottery. First, a bad marriage can literally be bad for you. Despite the common claim that married people are happier and healthier, new research indicates that being stuck in an unhappy union can gravely lower the state of your physical health as you get older.

A team led by University of Texas sociology professor Debra Umberson studied 1,049 continuously married people, who took surveys in 1986, 1989 and 1994 rating their health and marriage quality. While health ratings dipped for everyone over time, the slide was much faster for those who rated their marriages badly, especially as they got older. Married people did as a rule display better health than unmarried people, but despite this common trend the study decisively smashed the general assumption that any marriage was better for the health than no marriage. It also proved that the state of our health is linked to the quality of our relationships, and that good relationships become more important as we get older – marital stresses and strains affect us more and more as time goes by.[14]

The study suggested four reasons for these negative health effects becoming more pronounced in old age. Years of strain may slowly wear down health; age hampers the immune system, leaving elders more vulnerable to stress; older people are more likely to have chronic health problems that stress can aggravate; and older people may place greater emphasis on marriage as they lose other social ties. The team also cited research proving that people in distressed marriages are in poorer health than those in non-distressed marriages, and people in low-quality marriages show an even greater health risk than divorced people.

Another study, by UC Berkeley psychologist Robert W Levenson, PhD, attempted to work out why women's health suffered so much more than men's in a bad marriage, and came to the conclusion that women physiologically take on the characteristics of their partners in a kind of empathetic transference.[15] So if a husband gets angry and reacts with physical tension his wife will often take on that tension too, but she will have difficulty letting go of it as easily as he does, which means the increased pressure and stress can eventually have a negative knock-on effect on her health. A University of Pittsburgh study found that unhappily married women in their 40s are twice as likely as happily married women or women who've remained single to experience medical symptoms that could lead to strokes and heart attacks.[16]

I don't dispute that there may be some positive physical benefits to getting married, but without a doubt the potential for positivity depends on the strength and health of your marriage. If you think that just getting married is going to do you any good, you're sorely mistaken. The statistics and figures that constantly claim marriage as a health-giving cure-all seem to be focusing on good marriages, marriages that work rather than angry divorce-laden tragedies. As Stephanie Coontz says, 'Individuals in unhappy marriages are *more* psychologically distressed than people who stay single, and many of marriage's health benefits fade if the marriage is troubled.'[17]

Marriage can also have more obvious consequences for the female of the species, despite the hard work some of us are putting in to break through those glass ceilings. The statistics are encouraging – 73 per cent of young women in the United Kingdom say they want to keep working after they have a child even if they can afford not to, while 40 per cent of the country's professional jobs are held by women – but sadly, marriage still carries a certain degree of stigma for the working woman. Sexual discrimination is about more than calling your secretary 'honey' and trying to cop a feel at the photocopy machine. It may be illegal but that doesn't mean it's been wiped out, and it doesn't have to be about slobbering misogyny either.

Nancy, 28, has worked for a large Chicago PR firm for about three years. She loves her job but she's considering resigning because she's so incensed about not being promoted. It may sound petty but she has her reasons.

'When I started with the company I was the new young hotshot,' she says, 'and I loved it, it was great. I worked damn hard but that was fine because my work involved a lot of social gatherings and events. I met my fiancé Jay at a work function, and we clicked right away. He was totally cool with how seriously I take my job, and he's very into his career too, so it was fine. We moved in together quite quickly. Meantime work was going great and one of my bosses hinted that I was up for a big promotion. I was really happy, obviously, because there's a lot of competition and there are some guys in my department who are pretty good, really good actually. It was a big compliment. And I really wanted that promotion! My boss kind of made it clear that it was mine. Of course I told Jay and he was really excited too.

'He proposed a few weeks after that, which I was kind of expecting, and I said yes right away. I was really happy, and of course I told everyone at work. They were my friends, why wouldn't I? It felt totally natural and everyone was happy for me, and it seemed like life was working out just great. We didn't set a date or anything, there was no hurry, but we were really thrilled.

'About a month later a guy left our department. I thought it was going to be me who moved up to fill his spot till the last minute, but then my boss announced that the job was going to one of my male co-workers, a guy who was also pretty good but hadn't been expecting it at all. I was completely shocked and devastated. For a week I got really upset. I thought I'd misread the signs and figured I was being an idiot. Then Jay and I talked about it and I decided to confront my boss.

'I asked him really politely why I hadn't got the promotion. I phrased it like I wanted to know how I could do better. He was quite offhand and didn't say anything specific, except that he thought I'd lost focus in the last few weeks. And I knew he'd decided not to give it to me round about the time I said I was engaged. Maybe he thought as soon as I got married I'd quit and start having babies, which is nuts because he knows I'm a really hard worker.

'Jay never had any kind of negative reaction from his job. It was probably the baby thing – I don't think my boss wanted to promote someone who was going to run off on maternity leave in a year. I can understand that in a way but I'm *so* not like that, I was married to my job. The worst thing is he never actually admitted anything, and the guy who got the job was probably about as good as me, so I can't even complain. I love my job but I'm so angry now, I'm really thinking about quitting and going somewhere else. The whole place just leaves a foul taste in my mouth. You wouldn't think it would happen in this day and age, but it did and I know it. I just can't prove it.'

Nancy's situation is not unique. Thanks to stricter employment laws in most countries being a marriageable woman of childbearing age is no longer considered a crime against employee productivity, but nonetheless there are more subtle forms of discrimination that marriage engenders.

So yes, there may indeed be some discernible benefits to marriage. Perhaps you're one of the lucky ones who manages to pull off a passport scam with no personal or emotional consequences. Perhaps you squeeze a few pounds more out of the tax inspector. Perhaps your legal status changes, perhaps you have a little more money, perhaps your parents finally stop hassling you, perhaps you get that annoying stalker you used to date off your back. Perhaps you even get a legitimate excuse to buy that dress you've had your eye on. All of these things can happen. But all sorts of other things can happen too, troubles and traumas and downright tragedies, friendships and relationships destroyed, complications you could never have foreseen.

Perhaps you'll find out after two months that the woman you wed for her passport expects you to father her child, since you're, you know, married and all. Perhaps it'll be you who falls *Green Card*-ly in love with your non-romantic spouse only to have your heart stomped all over when they run off with the stunner from your local bar. The scope for drama is practically endless once marriage and all its attendant angst sidle into a perfectly functional situation. Signing that teeny tiny piece of paper may seem easy, fun and painless, but you're also signing up to a raft of potential disasters that, hidden as they are, are a lot less easy to spot than that little increase in your rebate statement. Ask yourself, is it really worth the risk?

Chapter Three

'We wanted a wedding'

For the longest time, I wanted a pony. I wasn't sure where I'd keep it or what I'd do with it but dammit, I wanted a pony. Called Midnight. In retrospect I'm fairly sure that what I really wanted was to ride Midnight to school so I could earn some much-needed cred with the pretty girls (there were a lot of John Wayne movies on TV when I was growing up). My vision of the whole situation ended with my triumphant arrival at the school gates and the awe-struck glances from perfectly turned-out princesses who'd never scoff at my glasses and braces again. Horseshit didn't enter into the equation, nor did waking up two hours before school to tack and clean; and that's not even considering the question of where you'd stable a pony in suburban Johannesburg in the 1980s.

My mother, fortunately, was no stranger to the weirdnesses of little girls, having been one, and did not get me a pony. If she had I would imagine that poor Midnight would have been loved to distraction for a year or so and then thrown over in favour of Luke Perry from *Beverley Hills 90210*, eventually ending up as dog food. (Luke Perry got superseded by Jim Morrison pretty speedily too, so it's a good thing no one tried to buy me one of him.)

People want things all the time. We want things because they are pretty or shiny or new or exciting, or because the kid down the block has one, or because we saw an advert that made us think they'd improve our lives, or because sexy people might like us more if we get one, or because Sharon Stone has one and wow, look at her. None of these are necessarily good enough reasons for us to be granted the things we're craving, especially when you take into consideration how swiftly desires change.

This is a peculiarly modern problem: there's always something newer, bigger and better waiting around the corner, some innovative toy or trick that will make us complete, that will make us happy, that will make it all worthwhile. Meanwhile we're choking our oceans and skies and condemning unlucky swathes of humanity who happened to be born in the wrong countries to virtual slavery, creating the objects of our desires and processing the waste they become as soon as something better is invented. This consumerist fever has tsunami'd its way into every aspect of modern life.

The point of getting married has been co-opted by the idea of 'having a wedding', the whole shebang, the big event, a multi-million-dollar industry that we pretend is fuelled by romance but is actually just another shameful example of corporate greed using our personal lives to make an absolute fortune. Having an 'event wedding' has become *de rigueur*, a rite of passage that all modern young people are expected to go through. The party with its attendant angst and cost and consequence has taken over the marriage. What with all the hysterical kerfluffle and emphasis on 'the big day' it's becoming too easy to forget that the purpose of the cake/dress axis of evil is not so you can have a nice photo album; it's about a lifetime commitment that comes with responsibilities, changes, constraints and a consequent loss of freedom (for all the positives it can add to your life).

If you're that desperate for a party, throw yourself a fabulous 21st, or 30th, or 40th. Have a 'Wahey, it's Tuesday' party. But a wedding is not just a party. There may well be some dancing involved, maybe a few embarrassing speeches and your divorced uncle leching over your bridesmaids, but that really isn't what it's about.

The linguistic theorist J L Austin came up with an oft-used way of classifying language in his 1962 book *How To Do Things with Words*.[1] Certain sentences could, he proposed, be performative: rather than just saying things they *do* things, they perform actions and make stuff happen in the real world. The most commonly used example of this is a priest or a registrar pronouncing a couple 'man and wife'. By saying these words he or she is also *doing* something, creating a legal marriage bond, a bond that at one point in human history actually dissolved the woman's legal existence and made her part of her husband. That's a serious business, a lot more serious that getting in some party poppers and doing the Macarena. A wedding is a lot like this. It's not just the party or the event that it may appear to be. It is performative, it affects the world, it *does something*. Too often couples are seduced by the glamour and the romance of having that all-important 'big day', and forget what it's actually there to do.

A question of ethics

So you want a wedding. Do you *need* a wedding? Would your relationship fall to bits if you didn't have one? Because if that's the case you should probably start dividing the presents now, before anyone gets too attached to the toaster. We all think we need things, but how frequently do we consider the effects those things have? Aside from our instant gratification, there are less visible consequences and repercussions – the rippling butterfly effect, if you will, that our behaviour has on more than our immediate environment.

Unless you've been living under a rock for the past five years or have worked as a scientific advisor to George W Bush, you will have at least some awareness of the fact that we're in planetary crisis. I hate to be the harbinger of doom – oh, all right then, I secretly quite enjoy it – but the human race is in deep, deep doodoo and we need to do something about it, fast. The exploding global population is consuming more resources and creating more waste than ever before. Our mechanised societies depend on burning fossil fuels, which release gases that get trapped inside the atmosphere and are slowly heating up the planet. We have deforested huge swathes of oxygen-producing land, killing off unimaginable numbers of species and ancient trees in our constant drive for expansion and progress. Up to 30 per cent of species on the planet will be at risk if temperatures climb by 1–4°C, while a 5°C increase will cause mass extinction.

These numbers sound like apocryphal horror movie stuff – but according to the UK government's Stern Review of 2006, our current rate of greenhouse gas emission means a more than 50 per cent chance that we're looking at a raise of up to 5°C.[2] Along with the species-wide devastation this would cause, it's equivalent to the difference between our current climate and the last ice age. The face of the planet would be irreparably altered, the conditions that gave rise to human life nothing but a memory. Think about the consequences of that for your annual skiing holiday.

A report published by the UN Intergovernmental Panel on Climate Change (IPCC) on 6 April 2007 was a grim forecast for human life in an era of global warming, with hundreds of millions of people suffering food and water shortages, thousands of species of plants and animals under threat, and floods, heat waves, storms and droughts increasing.[3] According to Rajendra Pachauri, chair of the panel that published the report, 'It's the poorest of the poor in the world, and this includes poor people even in prosperous societies, who are going to be the worst hit.' Humanitarian disasters like the 2004 tsunami and Hurricane Katrina will increase as the planet heats up and the polar icecaps melt. Populations already living in poverty will suffer first as their agriculture dissolves and their low-lying lands vanish, but the effects will eventually strike even the richest developed nations when food production hits crisis point.

Now it may seem like all this doom-crying is completely out of place in a book about marriage, but sadly that's not the case. Awareness of planetary crisis is no longer irrelevant *anywhere*; it's a challenge that has to be engaged with on every level of society. What we can't afford to do is wait for the politicians to sort it out. Until climate change becomes an electable issue they'll keep lining their pals' pockets and pleasing their pressure groups the same way they always have.

Scientists who worked on the IPCC report were actively pressured by representatives from various governments to soft-pedal their findings so as not to interfere with the demands of industry and that ravenous beast we call progress. Some of the report's authors even walked out of the talks in protest at how government agents – who had to approve the text before it could be published – were forcing them to water down their backed-up, scientifically proven findings of how we're jeopardising our species' future. So no, we cannot wait around for someone in power to fix this one for us. Because they don't care, not as long as oil revenue and tax from industry are pouring in. It's up to the little guy – and yes, that means *you*. We all need to become aware of the impact we have on the planet; we need to be conscious of every little decision and learn to minimise the harm we do while going about our fabulous, exciting, fast-food-laden Western lives.

Jonathan Porritt is chairman of the UK government's Sustainable Development Commission, its most senior advisor on sustainability policy. He paints a not very pretty picture of the effects of our rampant consumption habit, and suggests that if all 6 billion people on the planet sucked up resources at the same rate as those in the United Kingdom, it would take two more planet Earths to supply the energy, soil, water and raw materials required to keep them going. In an interview with the *Observer* in April 2007, Porritt said:

> I think capitalism is patently unable to go on growing the size of the consumer economy for any more people in the world today because levels of consumption are already undermining life support systems on which we depend – so if we do it for any more people, the planet will go pop.[4]

Yes, that's right, it is me and you and our shopping habits that are threatening, well, everything. Who knew that the greatest danger to the human race would come, not from aliens or evil geniuses or killer viruses, but from a plague of credit cards and consumer magazines?

In the context of all of this danger, it might be wise to stop and consider the effects of that great big wedding you're determined to have. Let's think about it for a moment. You want fresh flowers, right? Of *course* you do. A wedding just isn't a wedding without them. So where will you get them? From the florist, of course. And where we will the florist get them? From a magic garden out the back of the shop?

Those flowers have in all likelihood been flown over from Africa or South America using a ridiculous amount of aviation fuel and pumping carbon into the overstretched atmosphere. You can feel good about it, though, because people in faraway countries are making a living from growing them. Right? Not necessarily. Some aid workers have called the exploitation of flower plantation workers in Colombia the worst humanitarian crisis to hit the area in 50 years. And this in a country that's been riddled by civil conflict, the effects of the 'war on drugs' and sectarian violence across the board. Colombia supplies over half of the US fresh flower market.[5]

If you're buying in the United Kingdom, chances are your suppliers are either Dutch or Kenyan. So you'll go for the Dutch, obviously, to cut down on the air miles. But hang on: apparently it uses more carbon to heat and light those greenhouses in the Netherlands than it does to fly flowers all the way from Africa. Well, that answers that question – Kenya it is. But wait: many of Kenya's flower farms are located on the staggeringly beautiful 150 square kilometre Lake Naivasha. It won't be beautiful for very much longer, says environmentalist Margaret Otieno, because the lake could disappear altogether if exploitation of the water for flower cultivation continues.[6] There are also concerns that the fertilisers and pesticides being used by the flower growers could be banned substances, which is not very good news for the health of the workers. Do your flowers seem as uncomplicatedly pretty now?

What about, gentlemen, that great big rock you want to buy for your love – any idea where it came from? 'Conflict diamonds' are gems mined in war zones and sold, usually under the table, to finance an army or an insurgency. Many of the world's premium diamond producers are in Africa. Sierra Leone, Democratic Republic of Congo, Republic of Congo, Ivory Coast, Liberia and Angola have all been implicated in the illicit sale of conflict diamonds at some point between the 1970s and now. Many of these countries have cleaned up their acts since then, but nonetheless, there's a chance that the sparkly bling you have your eye on may not be as clean and shiny as it looks.

Conflict diamonds, plain and simple, pay for war. Diamonds and arms, arms and diamonds, and I don't mean the kind you put your watch on (unless we're talking about having those blown off). Keep in mind that Sierra Leone was the site of a civil war so bloody that thousands of civilians had their limbs hacked off with machetes by rebel or government forces. While the diamond trade may be doing its best to be accountable now, the ethics of buying them at all are still questionable.[7]

Then of course there's the question of transport, of the enormous numbers of miles racked up by your family and friends in getting to your wedding. Some of them may even fly in, which is the worst carbon crime there is. Plus unless you're rich enough to do it organically, or committed enough to do it yourself in locally sourced vegan fairtrade fashion, chances are the food for your meal will cost massively when it comes to fuel usage and carbon emissions. And since you're trying to get the best deals and your caterer buys cheaply in bulk, it's likely that your wedding will also be the best day of the lives of those poor chickens or cows who were reared in torturous darkness and pumped full of destructive chemicals before merciful death brought them to your table.

It's sad but it's true: in order to shop ethically on a large scale you need money. Few people can grow enough veg in their gardens or allotments to feed an entire wedding party, so even if you're generally concerned about the effects of your purchasing power those principles will probably have to go out the window on that special day. Which is not a very zen-like way of starting off married life.

The money trap

Going to all sorts of insane lengths to secure your dream wedding day will probably affect you personally, alongside the exacting toll it'll likely take on our poor benighted planet.

Perhaps you'll look more beautiful than you ever have before and your spouse will fall even more deeply in love with you, inspiring a future where you spend the rest of your lives skipping through fields of daisies holding hands with your perfect children. Which would be lovely. Or maybe, in all the excitement of trying to fit into a dress that's half a size too small, you'll fail to eat in the run-up to the big day, and then either fall asleep or throw up on yourself after your second glass of champagne at the reception. Maybe the in-laws will get into a fight, the best man will get off with your engaged best mate, your friends who used to be a couple will end up in a sobbing argument about whose fault it is that they broke up or one of the speechmakers will have a few too many celebratory whiskies and reveal something you'd both rather he didn't.

When you put families, alcohol, expensive clothes, adrenaline and highly charged emotions into a single room for an entire day, the chaotic permutations are endless. Don't forget that it's rarely moonlight and roses; no matter how carefully you plan things you can't regulate the responses of your loved ones or the tone on the day. There's a reason that weddings in films are so often scenes of unbridled pandemonium and disaster – it's a case of art imitating life, and probably being a poor reproduction.

However, more than these soap opera possibilities, one of the gloomiest (and usually unmentioned) consequences of the big white wedding is debt. The financial disaster that can decimate a relationship and a person's self-esteem begins horrifyingly often from their desire to start married life off with the biggest bang they can possibly afford (which usually means they can't). Because we all *deserve* the perfect wedding, don't we? We all deserve the most lush, ostentatious blow-out we can manage by any means necessary, even when said blow-out is the almost identical combination of clothing, music and food enjoyed by every other couple who gets married where we do. It's not about doing it the way we want, it's about doing it big and shiny and glossy and new and hang the consequences. Until, that is, the consequences come back to hang you.

Estimates vary when it comes to the cost of a wedding in the early part of the 21st century. But although there must be some people out there doing it on the cheap, that deviation is nowhere near as great as you'd expect it to be. In 2002, WeddingsUK.com worked out the average amounts according to these figures:

Bride's wedding ring	£200
Groom's wedding ring	£150
Groom's outfit	£150
Wedding dress	£700
Headdress and/or veil	£150
Bouquet	£75
Shoes and accessories	£125
Beauty treatments	£75
Bridesmaids' dresses	£500
Flowers	£200
Printing	£300
Transport	£300
Civil/church fees	£200
Photography	£400
Video	£400
Wedding cake	£200
Venue or marquee	£600
Decorations	£150
Reception	£2,000
Evening reception	£750
Drinks	£750
Entertainment	£500

Bride's going-away outfit	£150
Wedding night venue	£125
Honeymoon	£1,500
Wedding insurance	£50
Extra expenses	£300

That works out at £11,000. *Eleven thousand pounds*. That's US$21,701. Or €16,236. Or R155,145 for South Africans, NZ$30,050 for New Zealanders, 2,578,953 Japanese yen and 704,506 Thai baht. Whatever language you put it in it's a fearsome amount of money to spend on a single day. And that's not the half of it – those figures are a few years old and don't take into account special little extras like having an organ at the church, outfits for siblings and in-laws, buttonhole flowers for guests, cutesy name tags and take-home presents, thank-you cards, personalised napkins, a guest book, gifts for the retinue, the spiralling costs of stag and hen parties, press announcements, party planners' fees or accommodation for close family travelling in from out of town.

Now of that whopping great total, £1,475 is going on the bride alone. Well, gee. I hope she feels special, spending what is many people's monthly salary on her physical appearance for *a single day*. One would assume her husband is already prepared to marry her, so why this kind of excess is required I don't know, unless it's to impress people other than her intended.

Then there's the wedding night venue, by which time both bride and groom will probably be exhausted and ratty and ready for bed. Either they've had sex before, in which case it's not really necessary for her to have a whole new outfit to leave for their special hotel room in, or they haven't, which would be sad considering the nature of weddings today. If you've been saving yourself for your wedding night then you have two choices. You can either stay at the party, entertain your guests, enjoy the lavish spread that you're bankrupting yourselves to put on, and then finally leave, sweaty and tired and nowhere close to the flush of Mills & Boon perfection; or you can exit the party early and say bye bye to the few thousand pounds you've spent on it. (Someone else will probably have a good time.) And why on earth, can someone please explain, would you need a wedding reception and an 'evening reception'? Is one not enough in these grasping times we live in?

It's no picnic for the guests either. If, like me, you find yourself becoming slightly curmudgeonly at the prospect of throwing your hard-earned coppers away to celebrate one of your friends finally getting laid, then prepare to be shocked and appalled. Research from insurer Churchill claims that every time you attend a wedding in the United Kingdom you spend an average of £340.[8] That's a lot of shoes. And a cumulative £13.8 billion every year. Why, we could probably wipe out AIDS with that – but why bother when we can spend it on a pretty dress, some L-plates and a six-pack of alcopops!

The gift-giving side of things only comes to £60.31 of the average; transport is £82.40. We spend more on getting to our friends' ostentatious bashes than we do on, well, our friends. And, as will come as no surprise to anyone who's ever dared outdoors on a Saturday night in the normally laid-back British town of Brighton (girls morphed into shrieking harpies, blokes alternating between groping and vomiting), the largest chunk of this money – £90 – goes on the stag and hen nights, which these days can extend to an entire week of debauchery. Personally I've always found that Czech hookers and lap-dancing policemen are the perfect way to ease one into a serious long-term commitment. And that's not even counting the new clothes we buy, which everyone knows, have to at least attempt to outshine the couple getting married, even if only in acres of flesh exposed.

A later estimate from 2005 puts UK wedding averages at £15,244, including the reception (£5,000) and honeymoon (£4,500).[9] Now I don't know where these people are going on honeymoon, but I hope they're being fed grapes by beautiful boys in loincloths and taking potshots at the last of the world's snow leopards. Why would it be clever to blow that kind of moolah on a week or two, when you have a real life back in the real world that probably doesn't come for free? (If it does come for free, ignore everything I've said. In fact, give me a ring sometime, big boy.)

First you throw yourselves a great big party, then you give yourselves an amazing holiday. And why? Because you had the good fortune to fall in love with someone who also fell in love with you. That's it. The whole practice smacks of extreme arrogance – 'Look, aren't we special? Let's reward our love by making everyone we know come and celebrate it, and then let's reward ourselves by going off somewhere tropical to be smug at the natives too.' The whole tradition is turning into some kind of crazed one-upmanship whereby your life choices are only justified by how much money you're willing to spend showing them off.

The situation in the United States is similarly shocking, though it's not as simple to make blanket generalisations considering the vast size and economic disparity of the country. Still, thank God for those who try. These numbers are from a US wedding study conducted in 2002 and published online by www.costofwedding.com.[10]

Invitations etc	$381
Rehearsal dinner	$875
Bouquets and other flowers	$967
Wedding dress	$799
Photography and video	$1,814

Bride's headpiece/veil	$181
Favours	$241
Other bridal accessories	$186
Music	$900
Hair and make-up	$357
Clergy/church/chapel/synagogue	$297
Bridesmaids' outfits	$735
Limo hire	$577
Bride's mother's outfit	$236
Gifts for attendants	$510
Groom's outfit (rented)	$110
Printed matches and napkins	$112
Ushers' and best man's outfits (rented)	$575
Rings	$1,301
Reception	$7,630
Engagement ring	$3,576
Orchestra/band	$2,500

That makes for a grand total of $24,860, or £12,611. That's more than the UK average we saw for the same year, and it doesn't include a honeymoon. Raw deal! Great wedding, no holiday? Pfft, what's the point? You might as well keep living in sin.

These numbers, of course, are subject to change – OneWed.com puts it at $25,000, while the 2006 Wedding Statistics and Wedding Market Estimates Report, aimed at the industry, suggested the 2,271,910 weddings that were expected to take place that year would cost $26,800 a pop.[11] That's a 4 per cent increase on the previous year. They also predicted some impressive growth in the business, with the average reaching $31,400 by 2010. Somebody is making a lot of money and somebody is spending a lot of money.

In 2005 CNN reported a survey by the Fairchild Bridal Group indicating that national wedding expenditure was up to $125 billion, which is approximately the gross domestic product of the nation of Ireland, and a 73 per cent increase during the last 15 years.[12] Fairchild also pointed out just how quickly these prices have been rising. An engagement ring in 2005 cost $4,146, which is 39 per cent higher than in 1999; photography and video had a 103 per cent raise to $2,570; music for the ceremony or reception was $1,250, a 68 per cent raise; the rehearsal dinner had gone up 51 per cent to $1,153; and flowers, in a 45 per cent increase, were $1,121. CNN also suggested that 'nearly half' of marrying couples would overspend their budgets. And added to this is the question of location. If you live in New York you can expect to blow around $10,000 more than someone who has their wedding in the Midwest.

In 2002 the *Guardian* newspaper estimated the average cost of a UK wedding at between £12,000 and £14,000, with that price rising at more than twice the rate of inflation.[13] A study by stockbrokers Brewin Dolphin Securities found that the cost of a wedding at the start of 2007 was £19,595, and that 45 per cent of couples – that's 117,000 across the country – had no financial planning to pay for theirs.[14] The numbers of those with no payment plan are getting bigger, and the newly engaged are sticking their heads further and further in the sand to cope with the debt. In 2005 the BBC reported a survey by insurers ING Direct that suggested the average UK couple planned to spend £6,500 on their wedding, when the whole event eventually ended up costing around £16,500.[15] That's a pretty big mark-up for a pair of crazy kids, especially considering that just one in 20 weddings are fully paid for by the couple's parents. So the other 19 are scrimping, blowing their savings, taking out loans and running up terrifying credit card debts because they didn't realise how pricey it would get.

How do things like this happen? How is it possible to get yourself in so much trouble? Sadly it seems to be both easier and more common than you'd expect, what with the amount of pressure put on couples to make their weddings fit some preordained vision of perfection that's exactly the same as everyone else's. The costs start to mount up and the desire to do everything 'just right' becomes a financial rollercoaster, unless you're tough enough to ignore all the cries of doom that settle over every cheaper-than-average decision that you make.

Holly's summer wedding was quite out of the ordinary, held in a marquee in a field in the south of England with many guests camping, to suit her and her fiancé's easy-going lifestyle and eco-aware politics. Strong-minded and with a keen knowledge of green issues, she wasn't going to be pressured into changing her plans – which isn't to say that no one tried.

'It was very difficult to organise our wedding,' she says. 'Someone was telling me recently that he told his fiancé to just organise the whole thing herself. He said to her, "I want nothing to do with the organisation, everything you decide is fine." I think the men very often just step back and let the women get on with it. So that's a bit stressful.

'I knew exactly what I wanted which made it easier, but people did try to change my mind a lot. The caterer decided it would be nicer if we had the "proper" tablecloths and the "proper" chairs, and of course he knew someone who could provide them. I ignored him. A number of times. He kept saying, "It'll look bad, it'll look awful, I've seen it before and it looks terrible." But it didn't make a difference, no one noticed on the day.

'There's a very set idea of what a wedding should be like. Even my husband, who's the last person you'd expect to be like that, ended up agreeing with the caterer. I decided on white plastic chairs instead of the gold wooden ones with fluffy seats, and he was, like, "Ewwww, horrible." It's just because everyone thinks that things have to be a certain way, that because it's a wedding you have to sit on "proper" seats, but no one actually cared what they were sitting on on the day. I'm quite frugal and I think if I'd been less like that, it would have been easier for him to convince me that I was making terrible mistakes. At the end of the day we probably could have spent more than we did, but I don't like spending money like that, it's not necessary. It seems wasteful. We weren't scraping the barrel and we weren't specifically confined by money, we were confined by an awareness of what we didn't want to do.'

Let's just think, for a second, of all the other things we could be doing with this money. Other than solving third-world debt, getting plastic surgery for all the ugly people, buying ourselves the biggest shiniest computers in the world ever and maybe even finally purchasing that pony, we could be wangling our way out of debt and into financial health. And it's no joke – debt is a trap, a serious life crisis that unscrupulous financial providers lure us into.

Ever wondered why it's students, old people and the desperate who get bombarded with credit card ads, rather than nice middle-class types who could more easily afford to pay off some big expenses? They want us under their thumbs. They want to collect ridiculous interest payments from us, they want us to sign up for loans we can't afford to pay back because that way we'll end up giving them triple in repayments. These are not nice people. They're not offering you a wedding loan because they want you to have the best day ever. You could get married in a ditch for all they care as long as someone pays through the nose for it. Debt is a financial issue, of course, but it's also a moral one, tied to those questions I was asking before, about desire and consumerism and how much we really need to get by, and why we seem to end up with so very much more – and to be suffering for it.

Let's look at some horrible figures from the UK's 'money education charity' and pressure group Credit Action.[16] Total

UK personal debt at the end of April 2007 stood at £1,325 billion. Average household debt was £8,816, or £54,771 including mortgages. The average owed by every UK adult was £28,189 including mortgages, an increase of £165 since the end of March. The United Kingdom's personal debt is increasing by £1 million every four minutes. Total consumer credit card debt in April 2007 was £54.5 billion, and no wonder, since it was estimated in 2005 that banks and finance companies sent 1.26 billion pieces of junk mail offering services like loans and credit cards.[17]

According to APACS, the UK payment association, there are more credit cards than people in the country, 74.6 million cards against about 60 million people.[18] And, of course, it's not only the United Kingdom that's suffering. The average US household has 13 payment cards, including credit cards, debt cards and store cards. There are 1.3 billion payment cards in circulation in the United States. A 1992 Federal Reserve study showed that 43 per cent of US families spent more than they earned. As of 1995, 92 per cent of US family disposable income is spent on paying debts, up from 65 per cent in 1975.[19]

So what on earth are we doing? Spending and spending and spending to send ourselves into married life with a big beautiful bang, only to have married life dissolve under our feet when the creditors come a-calling. That £11,000 or £15,000 or £20,000 that we're merrily tossing away on a *single day* of our lives: shouldn't that money go on a deposit for a home? If we're so concerned about being married and being with that one person forever, shouldn't we be thinking just a little bit ahead to where we're going to live with him or her for the rest of our lives? Planning for a future together beyond the wedding day?

The average US house price reached $264,540 in October 2004, according to figures from the Federal Housing Finance Board, up from $243,756 in October 2003.[20] In April 2007 the

Department for Communities and Local Government put the average UK house price at £209,454, rising to £216,707 in England.[21] And that's on average. That's nothing special or amazing, it's just your bog-standard two up, two down, and hardly anything to get excited about. First-time buyers are spending an average of £158,097. A couple purchasing their first home will have to save up the equivalent of 81.8 per cent of their joint take-home salaries in order to raise the £32,784 they'll need for the up-front costs of buying a typical home.

Maybe part of the vision you have mapped out for your gloriously hazy post-wedding life involves rosy-cheeked children at play in your landscaped garden. Well, guess what, the cost of raising a child till its 18th birthday is now £180,137, or £23.50 a day, a 9 per cent increase on 2006. The question is not just why we're spending such extortionate amounts on our weddings but whether we can afford to have them at all. A young couple who don't own their own home and are just starting out in life together spunking away their savings or selling their souls to unscrupulous bankers for a great big party seems to be the height of irresponsibility – and not a very good indication of the kind of adult pairing they'll make.

Upsetting tales abound and we could spend all day on them, so I'll keep it to a minimum. Ellie is now 27, and at 23 she married Marcus after they'd been together for two years.

'I wanted a fairytale wedding,' she says. 'I always had these detailed ideas of what my wedding would be like. I played with my Barbies and gave them veils when I was young, the lot. Also I'm a complete girly girl and I loved the idea of the dress, the hair, all that. I told my mum and my sisters right after he proposed. They were just as excited as me, we'd all been waiting for this moment. Marcus didn't really get that I was as excited about the wedding as about marrying him, which I know sounds a bit shallow of me but it's the truth. It's not that

I didn't love him – I did, I do, he's absolutely the perfect man for me – but I had this wedding dream in my head. So he stepped back when it came to all the planning because he figured out quickly that I cared about it a million times more than him.

'Both our parents said they'd help out. We don't come from rich backgrounds but we were given a couple of thousand pounds by each of them. I just accepted it gratefully and didn't really consider how much of a stretch it was, especially for my mum, who's on her own and didn't have much to start with.

'I went way, way over budget. I was borrowing money from friends to pay deposits on the caterers. I took out two new credit cards. I bought my dress on credit: it cost almost £2,000. And everyone was egging me on, my family, my mother-in-law, my friends, all the people I was hiring to help make the dream happen. Everyone kept coming up with new ideas for how to make the day even better and I jumped every time.

'To be honest I felt at the time things were spiralling out of control but I was too caught up in it to get out. After a while I actually stopped feeling like the wedding was about me; it was about everyone else too, all their expectations.

'The only person I wasn't really thinking about was Marcus. I know that was my fault and selfish, but also it was a lot to do with the situation I was in. Everyone goes on and on about the bride, the bride, the bride as if there isn't a groom involved at all. So we kind of lost each other for a while.'

The wedding itself was, Ellie says, pretty much everything she and her cohorts had hoped for. But even dreams have consequences.

'We went to Cornwall on our honeymoon, very romantic, although I was kind of deflated and exhausted and trying not to think about how I was going to pay everyone back. Marcus kept saying he was so happy it went so well and so impressed I'd managed to pull it off. But on our second or third night we went for a posh dinner and when he went to pay the bill his credit card was declined. I'd "borrowed" it to pay for something a few months earlier and he hadn't checked the statement because he thought it hadn't been used.

'At that point I started having to admit I might have gone a bit overboard. He did some phoning around and found out just how overboard I'd gone and he couldn't believe it. He was completely shocked and saying stuff like, "I don't think I know you any more, how could I marry someone who'd do something like this?" I was just crying and crying. It was horrible, horrible, the worst fight ever, and it was our honeymoon.

'We went home the next day to start trying to sort out the mess. The money he had saved up for a house deposit went straight into paying back the banks. I phoned all the people I'd borrowed from to tell them I was going to pay them back. Everyone expected us to be in lovey-dovey land and here I was crying on the phone. But no one ever knew quite how bad it was, except Marcus, because it was a couple of hundred quid here and there from lots of different people.

'It was a horrible time and it's taken me so much work to sort it out. I stopped buying new clothes, did my hair myself and waxed my legs at home and stuff like that. I wanted to get it all sorted and prove I wasn't this selfish bitch. I know I have his respect back to a degree, but four years down the line we're still living in a rented flat and just starting to save up for a deposit again. House prices have gone even crazier so God knows how long it'll take us. I feel like such an idiot whenever I think about it. We don't even have any wedding photos up because our wedding was so beautiful and perfect and amazing, but we almost broke up because of it.'

Not all of us, fortunately, are seduced by the PR of big, expensive weddings, or even of weddings in general. Malka, a 35-year-old Londoner, happily flashes her engagement ring at the same time as admitting that she's in no rush to get married. 'We've been engaged for two and a half years,' she says. 'Originally I was really excited. We got engaged fairly quickly. I think at the time, when you're freshly in love, it seems like the most fantastic idea in the whole world to be making that commitment. But now that I've got the ring on my finger I think to myself, is it really necessary for the commitment to get married?

'Two and a half years ago I loved the idea of the dress and the big event, I was quite extravagant in my plans. Now I don't want to spend that much money. I think it's rubbish – why spend all that money when you could use it for something else?

'I want to make a commitment but I don't think that marriage is the be all and end all of whether I'm going to have kids and whether I'm going to stay with this guy. I've had my doubts. I think when you're not madly in love you do have doubts, because then you think, if he isn't the one I'd end up having to divorce him, and that sounds horrible. Your romantic ideas override the practical ideas in the beginning but then reality kicks in. It's so easy to marry someone when you're in the throes of love, but then you can find yourself, a year later, with a husband and a mortgage, deeply in debt, with a kid even, and that's not freedom.

'If it does go ahead with me I will be excited and I'll see it as a very social day. But I think I'll be happy with just a few friends.'

Marriage à la media

It's hardly surprising that we're all obsessed. Weddings have, as I say, become big business, and if there's one thing big business is good at it's advertising. The amount of press coverage leading up to some recent celebrity weddings has been exceeded only by the completely bonkers nature of the weddings themselves. And as we know by now, whatever famous people do, the rest of us will soon copy, for if we ever had free will the incessant bombardment of multiple TV channels and the pumping soundtrack to modern life have effectively shut it down. We shuffle along like a slack-jawed herd of grazers, slurping our Coke Zeros and mumbling incoherently at our TV screens. (It's enough to make you wonder whether *The Matrix* wasn't a fair and balanced documentary piece.)

A poll commissioned by the *Guardian* newspaper in the UK in 2002 showed that the number of people who believed marriage was becoming fashionable again had doubled since 1999, with 41 per cent of those asked believing the institution was getting 'cool'. The same poll showed that almost one in three 25- to 34-year-olds, a quarter of late 30-somethings and 23 per cent of 45- to 54-year-olds were single, which is bizarre considering that these were the same respondents bleating about marriage suddenly being hip.[22] Where could the disparity have come from? It's partly down to 'the in-depth coverage of Posh-and-Becks-style showbiz weddings in magazines such as *Hello!* and *OK!*,' says the *Guardian*. Yup, famous people. They're doing it so it must be good; and boy oh boy, are they doing it. The amount of money these people are forking out so the rest of the world can gawp in envy is mind-boggling.

Elizabeth Hurley, spokesmodel, celebrity, designer and occasional actress, is still best known for wearing a skimpy dress to her then-boyfriend Hugh Grant's *Four Weddings and a Funeral* premiere, then later getting pregnant by a Hollywood cad and carrying it off with dignity. Dignity was in somewhat short supply in March 2007 when she married her current paramour, Indian businessman Arun Nayar. (What does that description even mean? Does anyone know? Or is he Liz's equivalent of a handbag, in which case it hardly matters?) First the happy couple wed at a 'private ceremony' in Sudeley Castle in the English Cotswolds. The low-key sounding civil ceremony was speedily trumped by the reception the next day, which was sold to *Hello!* for an obscene sum of money. Liz looked very pretty in her white dress.

But that wasn't it, oooooooh no. Next the couple jetted off to India so they could have a traditional wedding there, presumably so Arun's mum didn't feel left out. After their arrival in Jodhpur and three days of pre-wedding parties, including a midnight game of cricket and an evening of dance and music at Naghaur Fort, they had a splendiferous traditional Hindu ceremony on the Friday night, complete with guests in saris and the groom arriving on a white horse.

A fight broke out outside the venue between Liz's zealous security and some desperate paparazzi snappers, but nonetheless the couple's privacy remained intact. Except for that issue of *Hello!*, naturally. But that hardly counts. And it's not like her adoring public missed out, with almost every news outlet in the United Kingdom, from the venerable BBC to the rascally tabloids, featuring blow-by-blow coverage of every stage of the epic event, including front-page photographs of a sometime model marrying a businessman. You have to wonder how many people would have had to die in Iraq or Darfur to merit that sort of coverage.

Elizabeth's intercontinental fiesta, while certainly impressive, is dwarfed by reports of Tom Cruise's wedding to Katie Holmes. The beautiful 15th-century Odescalchi Castle was the locale for the 18 November 2006 event, which saw 150 A-est of the A-list guests, including Will Smith, some Beckhams, Jim Carrey, Jennifer Lopez, John Travolta, Kirstie Alley and many eminent – for which read loaded – Scientologists descend on the small town of Bracciano near Rome. Just, you know, 150 of their closest friends. Famed tenor Andrea Boccelli serenaded the guests (do the Cruises even like opera, or is high culture the wedding theme *du jour* for people in weird religions?), who feasted on four courses and a white chocolate wedding cake. Giorgio Armani designed Mrs Cruise's gown, a diaphanous confection covered with Swarovski crystals. Her wedding-night lingerie alone reportedly cost $3,000. But money is no object to people so madly in love – while the ceremony was short the couple's kiss apparently went on for a cringe-inducing three minutes.[23] And, you know, they're actors, so of course they meant it.

Catherine Zeta-Jones and Michael Douglas, who wed on 18 November 2000,[24] sued *Hello!* for £2 million, claiming stress, loss of earnings and damage to their careers after the magazine breached their privacy by sneaking photographers into their reception and then printing the photos. So far so fair. Except for the little detail that the couple had already sold the rights to the event to rival celeb rag *OK!*, and the *Hello!* scoop endangered their deal. I suppose deciding which upmarket tabloid gets to print intimate photos of the 'most important day of your life' is a form of privacy in some lights. Given that three security firms, the New York police department and the fire brigade were involved in policing the event at the New York Plaza Hotel, it's amazing that the offending snaps got taken at all. The wedding reportedly cost £1.5 million, including £500 catering per guest and £100,000 on her dress, with *OK!* stumping up a million for the rights. Attendant luminaries included Sean Connery, Jack Nicholson, Sharon Stone, Michael Caine, Christopher Reeve and Danny DeVito. Now that's entertainment.

Elton John and David Furnish celebrated their historic civil partnership, one of the first under the UK's new 'gay marriage' law, in typically impressive style in December 2005. While the ceremony was a small, private affair (except for the hundreds of fans and photographers who lined the road outside the registry office), the $1.75 million reception in the grounds of their Windsor mansion was most decidedly neither. The 700-strong guest list included Boris Becker, Liz Hurley (we know she loves weddings), the Osbourne family, Ringo Starr, Michael Caine, Sting, Donatella Versace, Claudia Schiffer, George Michael, Victoria Beckham, Greg Rusedski, Helena Bonham Carter, Nick Faldo and a veritable who's who of minor UK failed pop royalty.

Then of course there was the wedding to end all weddings: shy and retiring pop star Victoria Adams, of a little-known outfit called the Spice Girls, and a lad named David Beckham who does something with a ball. They married at Luttrellstown Castle in Ireland on 4 July 1999, having – yup, you guessed it – sold the rights for £1 million to a celebrity magazine. This particular wedding attracted as much ridicule as it did envy, mainly for the completely astounding sight of bride and groom regally enjoying the scene before them from matching gold thrones. Subtle.

Liza Minnelli and David Gest spent $3.4 million on celebrating their short-lived marriage. Brad Pitt and Jennifer Aniston – spent a million, now split up. Paul McCartney and Heather Mills – also spent a million, also split up. It's not a very wise investment. But as long as they keep doing it we'll keep buying the magazines they sell the rights to, oohing and aahing over the dresses and the bridesmaids' pumped-up cleavage, and hoping, nay, dreaming of a superstar wedding of our very own.

The real marriage blues

Let's say you choose to ignore my perfectly pitched advice and careful injection of guilt, and go ahead with the damn thing anyway. Will it make you happy? Oh really? Are you sure about that? It might sound like the title of a trendy chick-lit novel, but post-nuptial depression, or PND, is a new buzzword among therapists and counsellors who are seeing increasing numbers of newlyweds who are neither happy nor euphoric. Just the opposite, in fact.

While no specific research has been done into the condition, anecdotal evidence thus far suggests that it can strike when the excitement and glamour of the wedding day are over and bride and groom suddenly find themselves dropped back to earth with an enormously big bump. They've spent months and months planning for a single day, looked more attractive than ever before, been completely the centre of attention and often focused all their energies so intensely on the wedding that its finality can feel like losing a job, suddenly being deprived of the main thing they spent their days doing. And then there's the shame – how dare you feel anything less than wonderful when you've just had this massive event, this great experience that you and, possibly, many of your loved ones, have turned yourselves inside out to arrange? How dare you be so ungrateful, so demanding? As any sufferer of depression will know, burying it under layers of guilt and angst really doesn't help.

According to Monica Lanman, a psychotherapist at the Tavistock Marital Studies Institute in London, 'Admitting that you feel wretched after so much time, money and attention has been spent on you is too hard for most people to do. Compounding guilt with depression makes it less likely that people will seek help, which can make recovery even harder.'[25]

Then there are the physical, mental and financial stresses of having a wedding, where participants often burn the candle at both ends to get everything done and direct all their energies into making it come together as perfectly as possible. Rather than euphoria, common post-wedding responses are exhaustion and the attendant crash it brings when the bubble of anticipation bursts. Plus, of course, people who have invested this much care and attention in their wedding day are often expecting marriage itself to be a picnic, a romantic curative for all of their previous ills (whereas we know that marriage is often stressful, demanding, tiring and – go on, let's admit it – boring).

Linda Blair is a clinical psychologist at the UK's University of Bath. She says, 'The syndrome can sound insignificant but, if it's not dealt with, it can slip into real depression and last indefinitely. Post-wedding blues are becoming more and more common, not because marriages have become worse but because people's expectations of a one-off solution to their problems are higher.'[26]

Our romanticised view of marriage is expanding beyond the boundaries of rational thought, and our belief in this outdated institution defies all logical explanation. Even as divorce rates soar and singletons increase in number, it seems like many of us are still clinging to that romcom-induced hope that all we need is a cake and a dress and someone to stand next to for a day, and everything will, somehow, be OK. It's a false and deluded ideal, and there's little wonder that so many newlyweds are struggling horribly with the demands and failures of their lives, with the expectations they had and the beliefs they held so dear. Because no matter how much money and time you spend on it a wedding is still just a wedding, just a single day, and after that there's the whole of the rest of your life to get through.

PND seems to affect women more than men, presumably because in the majority of cases brides still have more to do with organising their weddings than grooms, and so have more to lose when the magic carpet is removed and they're forced to realise that they're not the fairytale princess any more. The day they've been waiting for has gone in a flash and it's now time to stop having fun. Some people go into marriage with the idea that, somehow, that one special day will miraculously make them from two into one, that the vows will become the truth all on their very own, without any work from them.

Phillip Hodson, a fellow of the British Association for Counselling and Psychotherapy, points out that there is no specific research into PND and it is likely to be exacerbated by having a depressive nature or a history of mood swings. But nonetheless, coming down to earth with an almighty thump after a big wedding is a pervasive problem. He says:

> Newlyweds think that there'll be no more rowing and everything will be great. You risk depression if you marry the wrong person or for the wrong reason – youthful folly, to have sex, because you were drunk in Las Vegas, because she's pregnant or to please his mum – and also because marriage involves procreation. There is evidence to show that the arrival of the first child causes a deterioration in the marital relationship which doesn't entirely recover (if it does, 20 years is another peak time for divorce) until the last child has left home.
>
> The depressing nature of marriage also has a lot to do with going from a state where you are permitted as much freedom and fun as you want to its exact opposite. You go from pleasing yourself and spending your own income to suddenly having to be grown up and do things like have mortgages and save. Some people say that you're freer once you've found the person you want to marry because you can relax with your loved one, and while there may be a spiritual dimension to this on the whole I disagree – it's a very controlling view and assumes that the world won't throw unexpected things at you.
>
> There is also the fact that marriage is bigger than the individuals embarking on it – and some people, from one third to a half of all new entrants, are doomed to split because they have

> too little in common to sustain them when the honeymoon effect has worn off. Opposites may attract – we can fancy anyone – but only similars can really stand each other in the long run. In reality, nobody gets married to get divorced. If we had the same rate of casualties in Iraq as we do in marriages we'd be out of there. It might work better if people were less starry-eyed, and for that I blame the bridal industry. The real life-changing event is not the wedding, it's the child. The wedding is just another day.[27]

It has the veneer of one of those silly modern afflictions that are invented by glossy newspaper supplements to give rich Western women an excuse for their misery, but PND seems to be a lot more universal than that. Aruna Broota is a clinical psychologist in New Delhi, India, and has seen a growing number of new spouses of both sexes experiencing the symptoms in recent years. 'It's the first two years of marriage that are really difficult,' she says. 'The responsibilities, the feeling of being tied down combined with very high expectations often put too much pressure on the relationship.'[28] The code of silence that surrounds the condition – the same code that dictates that every newlywed must be madly, ecstatically happy – can be just as damaging as PND itself. Over and over people who've experienced PND say the same things. Why did no one warn me? Why didn't I know this could happen? Why wasn't I told? These are the almost-casualties of our dearly cherished belief that newlyweds must be living in a dream of marital bliss, that marriage itself is such a panacea that nothing can possibly be wrong with them.

The following is a testimonial written by a woman who calls herself Emily S from the website Feminist Mormon Housewives – hardly a typical platform for spoiled whining.

> On my wedding day, blissfully happy though I was, I cried and cried. I made it almost all the way through our small reception/luncheon, high on happiness and buttercream frosting, but as I watched my best friend and her sisters prepare to take their leave to go back to a life to which I no longer belonged, the floodgates began to open . . .
>
> I don't think I've ever read or listened to a discussion of that depressive phenomenon – much like buyer's remorse – that often (at least, according to my word-of-mouth research) descends upon us after marriage. It isn't a lack of love for our spouses, it's not a lack of gratitude for the blessing that is finding your match, and it's not just a surface discomfort. For me, it was more of a fundamental sadness for the loss of my former self, a deep-seated worry that I wouldn't be able to navigate these new waters (no matter how much I loved my first mate), and a deep, dark, secret doubt whether I even wanted to navigate those waters anymore. I was appalled at myself. I thought I must surely be the most ungrateful wretch ever to walk the earth.
>
> It wasn't until I had a very open talk with my older sister, that I realised I wasn't alone in feeling this way. I listened to her talk about how she sometimes resented her husband in the early days of their marriage, and how she regretted missing out on some opportunities because she'd married young. Both of us are married to gems among men but both of us had felt so trapped, angry, sad, doubtful, depressed. I have since found that it wasn't just us, either.

So what are we looking at here? People feeling severely depressed just days after their dream weddings and hiding their anguish in shame. Couples diving into married life laden with the kind of debt that may hound them for the rest of their days. Fame-crazed celebrities hysterically blowing millions to ensure the gauchest, most extreme, over the top, self-aggrandising marital events imaginable, and mindless 'civilians' at the bottom of the food chain doing their best to imitate. Mountains of waste and carbon emission, profligate, thoughtless, careless, damaging, self-obsessed 21st-century consumerism, buying more and more and more, and to hell with the consequences for our earth or our souls or our selves. Not quite the picture of perfection you see in *Hello!*, but these, ladies and gentlemen, are some of the hidden costs that your $5,000 wedding planner might somehow forget to mention.

Chapter Four

'It's just what you do'

There's a popular saying I'm rather fond of that suggests the things you regret are those you didn't do, not those you did. It's generally uttered alongside the kind of pearls of wisdom that dictate that no one lies on their deathbed saying, 'I wish I'd gone to work more.' There are many ways to have an interesting life. Just because you're not the kind of person who would throw it all away and run off with a stripper named Scarlet doesn't mean you have to do everything the same way everyone else does.

We are each given one single solitary life (except Buddhists, who get loads, but some of them are as insects and hardly count), and we have to make that life work for us. I'm not suggesting that we all toss off the shackles of convention, jack in our jobs, change our names to Badger and live in caravans. That life may suit some free-thinking souls but most of us would find it a bit, well, weird. What we can do is learn from those who tread the less common paths, get some hints from the sense of freedom and self-regulation that they have. And I don't mean making friends with the dreadlocked guy who sells magazines on the corner (although I've found that dreadlocked guys who sell magazines on corners are invariably excellent company). I mean thinking, much as it pains me to invoke management-speak, outside the box.

I'm talking about making choices that aren't necessarily the obvious ones and aren't regulated by the drive to conform, to do exactly as we're told, to make our lives fit the same precise pattern as the lives of everyone who shares our social, economic and racial milieu. Because the standard one-size-fits-all programme really doesn't, in the final analysis, fit all at all, and many of us find it constraining and restrictive. Think about it – it's hardly a thrill a minute. You're born, you go to school, then maybe college or university if you're lucky, get a job, get married, have a kid, have another. You get a better job, buy a bigger house, the kids leave, you retire and rattle around for a while with the spouse you haven't really spoken to in years, you get old, move to a home, and with a whimper not a bang that's it. That's *it*. That's all the time we get. And here we are spending it on doing the 'right thing', on sticking with the herd and keeping our heads down, not making a fuss, not standing out, not taking risks.

Humans are pack animals and it's in our instinctive nature to do what's best for the majority, to keep paying those bills so our governments can function, buying those products so big business can flourish, teaching our sons and daughters to do exactly what we did in exactly the same way. But the pack mentality hasn't evolved at the same breakneck speed as society.

Perhaps when we lived more tribally it was important not to break with tradition and to follow expected paths, so the others in your group would know what you were doing and there were no dangerous surprises that could jeopardise the safety of the whole. If everyone hunted the same way then everyone could hunt together and food would be easier to find. The world doesn't work like that any more – unless you're defining the world by global capitalism, which is very pleased when we all behave identically because it makes it easier to market toilet paper.

Global capitalism does not, however, often have the good of the species at heart, at least not the good of the part of the species that's not Western and wealthy. Now I'm not advocating complete selfishness or a belief that what concerns the rest of humanity has no bearing on us. I don't think we should all hang convention out to dry since, hey, we're not hunter-gatherers any more so why bother? What I am suggesting is that mindless conformity does no one any good. The 'because' answer just isn't valid for thinking 21st-century human beings.

'Why are you getting married?' 'Because.' 'Why are you taking out an enormous home loan?' 'Because.' 'Why are you insulting the foreign guy?' 'Because.' 'Why are you voting for that party?' 'Because.' One man walks unswervingly past a side street where a woman is screaming; most of the people who come after him will walk past too.[1] One person stops and runs in to see if he can help and he'll be followed by a crowd. The converse effect of the deadening urge to do what everyone else is doing and not draw attention to ourselves is the sense of freedom that comes when one person steps out of line, and we see that and realise we can follow him. We can even go in a completely different direction.

The psychology of conformity

There are all sorts of pressures and pushes that come into play when we're negotiating our way through life and trying to find the correct or appropriate way of behaving. Dr George Boeree, of the psychology department of Pennsylvania's Shippensburg University, outlines four types of conformity that can affect our feelings and choices.[2]

The first is *unconscious and internalised*. It's probably learnt in childhood and is made up of social norms that we don't often seriously question, just assuming that that's how things are and that's obviously how things are meant to be because, well, it works, doesn't it?

The second type is a *conscious choice* that happens when we voluntarily join a group. Just watch any high school kid – as soon as they acquire a new group of friends that group's uniform and lingo of choice will be speedily adopted. In its most drastic form, such as when people get involved with new religions, this is called conversion.

Third, we conform *when we're forced to*, which is often called compliance. We do what everyone else is doing because of the threat of punishment if we don't or reward if we do, and it feels significantly less voluntary.

The fourth and most interesting type Dr Boeree calls *defensive conformity*, actions that are 'somewhat conscious' and 'not quite voluntary', usually brought on by social anxiety – 'fear of embarrassment, discomfort at confusion, a sense of inferiority, a desire to be liked'. The field of social psychology separates this into two distinct types. The first is known as *informational influence*, and happens when a person is in doubt about how to behave and so turns to the members of his or her group to get the information required for the decision. This is most common in three circumstances:

- when a situation is confusing and it's difficult to tell which would be the right way to turn, we look to our peers and follow their lead;
- when a crisis happens and a decision needs to be made fast, we follow what others do to calm our fears of making the wrong choice in the small amount of time available;
- when in the presence of experts whose specialised knowledge we believe to be superior to our own, we find their actions worth imitating.

This kind of social influence often leads us to internalise the paths we've chosen to follow, so that no matter how we felt about them at first we eventually come to genuinely believe in them. There have been many interesting experiments to examine how people cope in situations like these, including identifying 'criminals' in a line-up. One group in this experiment was told that their input was hugely significant to legal research, while the other group knew it was just a trial. The first group, who were placed in a crisis situation by the emphasis on the importance of their choices, conformed to what the others in the group were doing 51 per cent of the time, compared with 35 per cent in the control group. Put people in a situation that they think is life-changing and vital and they may be more likely to do what everyone else around them is doing. And, in many cases, they'll internalise this choice, so they end up convincing themselves it was what they believed all along.

The second type of defensive conformity behaviour is known as *normative social influence*, and occurs when one conforms in order to seek acceptance from a peer group. This was famously illustrated in the 1950s by Solomon Asch, a professor of psychology at Swarthmore College, Pennsylvania.[3]

Asch gave his group of subjects, all but one of whom had been briefed on what to choose, a 'vision test'. This involved being shown a card with different-length lines and being asked questions such as which line was the longest and which were the same length, or being told to match the length of one of the lines on the card with a line on another card. They were questions that the students who had been briefed would answer incorrectly. Asch initially assumed that conformity would be lessened in such a clear situation – it was obvious which line was longest – but he was surprised by his results. Seventy-six per cent of participants conformed on at least one trial. In an average one-third of the time, people agreed with what the others in the room had said even when it was obviously wrong.

Even when they gave the correct answer rather than the majority answer, many participants got very upset and found the experience highly uncomfortable. And, interestingly, when told later that they'd got it wrong, most participants blamed themselves, their bad judgement or 'poor eyesight'. No one blamed the experiment for leading them astray. This suggests that when we make bad decisions because we desire to conform to our peer group we're likely to lay the blame at the feet of a personal deficiency, something that's wrong with us rather than something wrong with the group. Others admitted that they'd chosen as they had because they didn't want to 'feel silly' by standing out, which ties with psychologist Rom Harré's suggestions that a secondary human need is for social respect, the desire to avoid criticism.[4]

Human beings have a tendency to make decisions based on this drive to avoid at all costs looking ridiculous in front of others. What these studies show is that the pressure to fit in with those around us can be so strong that it leads us to deny the clear evidence of our own eyes. In later experiments Asch brought in others who disagreed with the group consensus, and found that just one dissenting voice – even when it also gave an incorrect answer – led to a notable increase in the subjects' willingness to disagree with the majority conclusion.[5] This is known as social support. Unlike the internalisation that comes with informational influence, normative social influence generally results in public compliance, doing or saying something without meaning it.

Dr Catherine Butler, a London-based clinical psychologist, explains:

There's something in communication theory called coordinated management of meaning that maps out how we make meaning of events. If you apply that theory to marriage, you have the marriage in the centre and then you have layers of meaning that are 'storied' around that event. Some of those layers may contradict each other and some may support each other. Some of the layers are, loosely, culture and religion, and obviously with weddings those are going to be a really major influence.

For many people it's about when you get married, who to, all those sorts of things. And then you have family stories that may contradict some of those religious stories, for example that you have to be together for life: you may have parents who've been divorced or the aunt who never got married. So you have family stories about marriage and then you have relationship stories about marriage in terms of your current beau, the stories you may both bring, because you're both bringing your individual cultural and religious stories so you're both trying to work out a way how those would match up – how long do you need to be dating before you move in, who proposes to who, is it around gender norms. And then you'd have your individual, personal stories that you've developed as a separate entity from those other stories. You might have developed, say, political beliefs that affect your view of marriage, you might have different opinions of ownership.

So when an event happens like marriage, whether it's your own marriage or someone else's, all those different layers of meaning will be triggered to make sense of it – is this a good thing or a bad thing, is she marrying the right person, the wrong person? The way the theory works is that for whatever reason some of those layers will be more powerful or more dominant than other layers. Maybe you've rediscovered your religion, so that might be a really strong layer, or you might be

> of a certain age and want children so the whole family story will become more dominant, but it's very much the idea that all different layers may be either supportive or contradictory of each other, and as multiple complex human beings we can hold all those different meanings.
>
> There's also a question of gender identity in marriage, what it means to be a man or a woman. A lot of that is bound up with formalising our relationships. Especially for women: I think for men there's an alternative gender identity that they can live, the lad, the playboy, although that can't go on forever. People get married because it 'makes' them into a woman or a man, it defines them as their gender. I think that the religious layer is very strong too; if it was just about finding a mate and breeding, then why bother with getting married?[6]

What all of this boils down to is that it can be very difficult to make rational decisions. We have the entire weight of our cultures, societies and peer groups coming to bear on us every time we're faced with a choice, and as we've seen, the human tendency to conform is enormous. Getting married in your early 20s and having your first child by 25 may work out just fine for the 15 of your friends who've done it, but that doesn't mean it'll suit you. We are each made up of intricate layers of meaning, belief and experience, and no matter how similar we may seem to the people in our peer group, we're not the same as them. Making choices based on what everyone else does, no matter how tempting and comfortable, can be an enormous mistake.

The assumption that similar backgrounds make for similar characters just isn't true; witness the sheer variety of people in any small community. If it was true that growing up in the same place and with the same beliefs made us the same, then small towns would all be made up of alpha couples who shared equal status instead of boasting a soaring range of the isolated, the disliked, the morally questionable and the downright odd alongside upstanding citizens, firemen and Sunday school teachers.

We each negotiate our own paths, finding a way to make all the diverse layers of our lives add up, and those layers are not identical for anyone. But yet when we sit in a room with a group of people who seem to come from the same place as us and listen to them all make a choice that's clearly wrong, much of the time we'll agree with them to keep the peace, to keep our heads down, to avoid humiliation. We trust the mentality of the pack more than we trust our own eyes and minds, our self-knowledge. This is known as 'groupthink', and was codified by the psychologist Irving Janis, who explained it thus: 'A mode of thinking that people engage in when they are deeply involved in a cohesive in-group, when the members' strivings for unanimity override their motivation to realistically appraise alternative courses of action.'[7]

A classic case of groupthink was the disastrous 1961 Bay of Pigs invasion, when President Kennedy's government settled on a plan to arm and train a group of Cuban exiles to return home and overthrow Fidel Castro. The plan was full of holes and could probably never have worked but none of Kennedy's advisors spoke out against it, afraid perhaps of breaking majority consensus and cohesion. No one wanted to upset the President, no one wanted to isolate himself, no one wanted to be the one who disagreed with everyone else, no one wanted to point out that the emperor had no clothes on, and so the attack went ahead and was a huge embarrassment. The consequences of sticking with a group decision that overrides your personal opinion can be disastrous.

Religion and the marital imperative

Questions of conformity are only half the issue because they depend on unconscious factors, feelings and desires that lurk within our minds but are often unspoken and seldom acknowledged. The pressure can become intolerable when these conformist urges are compounded by external forces, actual verbalised coercion that attempts to push us into a mould we may not feel comfortable with. It's bad enough when you look at everyone in your peer group and they're all doing exactly the same thing; the feelings of shame and anxiety that can stem from a refusal to follow the group can be crushing. And then added to these covert motivations are actual, tangible overt pressures, when the people around us, or the people we respect, or those who dominate our social groups, make it clear that we're expected to behave a certain way and no other performance will do.

Religion is one of those pressures that pushes people into making decisions they wouldn't otherwise make. It has subtle and insidious effects on the culture – the idea of a marriage ceremony is a fundamentally religious one – and there is, if we look closely enough, an element of hypocrisy in so many people rushing off to be married in the sight of a god they don't even believe in. The enormous effect of monotheism on Western culture is undeniable. Most of our rules, norms and unquestioned social standards can be traced to the Christian Church at some point or another, and whether they're taken as metaphors or as historical truths, the founding tales of Christianity – a virgin birth, a human child of the divine and a resurrection – are concepts many of us would be uncomfortable with or deeply scathing of in any other context. Examining the mythology a religion is based on can often, if one does not have faith in its basic precepts, throw up some startling contradictions and oddities in that religion's heart; and yet we often to fail to interrogate the sway it has over modern morals and mores.

The Old Testament is littered with examples of marriages that would shock and appal modern religious leaders. Just look at Abraham, the great patriarch, fathering a son on his concubine Hagar and then one on his wife Sarah, spurring his Jewish and Muslim descendants into centuries of conflict. King Solomon, the wisest of them all, had 'seven hundred wives, princesses, and three hundred concubines' (1 Kings 11:3). Even Moses had both his wife Zipporah and an unnamed Ethiopian woman he'd married. In contrast to this marital abundance early Christianity was no fan of even conventional marriage, viewing it as a necessary evil. We saw in Chapter One that the Church thoroughly disapproved of romantic love that distracted parishioners from their rightful devotion to Jesus, but more than this, the Lord Himself did not endorse marriage among his followers, insisting that spouses and family took a distant second place after the burning need to prepare people for the coming of the kingdom of God. 'If any man come to me and hate not his father, and mother, and wife, and children, and brethren, and sisters, yea, and his own life also, he cannot be my disciple' (Luke 14:26).

In *Marriage: A History*, Stephanie Coontz writes, 'What distinguished early Christianity from Judaism in its approach to marriage and family was the belief that the kingdom of God was close at hand, and people must therefore break with worldly ties to prepare for the imminent arrival of that kingdom.'[8] Instances of the Bible sermonising against marriage abound. 'He that is unmarried careth for the things that belong to the Lord, how he may please the Lord: but he that is married careth for the things that are of the world, how he may please his wife' (I Corinthians 7:32–34). And though early priests and popes agreed that to marry was better than to be preoccupied with lust they still questioned the necessity of the institution, as marriage involved sex, and sex was always, no matter what the circumstances, sinful.

Of course, expecting 21st-century Christians to live literally by 2,000-year-old principles would be insane. Like any living culture Christianity has grown and changed and its central tenets have changed with it. We could expect nothing less of a religion that wants to survive, and it would be curmudgeonly and unfair of me to castigate modern Christians for not sticking to the exact letter of a holy book that, like most holy books, contains its own contradictions and inconsistencies.

I'm not suggesting that anyone with pretensions to Christianity should immediately swear off the opposite sex and move to a nunnery or monastery, whichever's appropriate. What I am suggesting is that we take the interpretations of religion with a pinch of salt, because these change over the centuries to suit the social mores of the day as well as the motives of the priests or kings who are making the rules. As can be seen by this example, there is a lot of ambiguity in the current right-wing conservative insistence on the holy trinity of 'marriage, the family and family values' as the core beliefs and driving forces of Christianity. Marriage was not originally 'a good thing' for Christians, but now elements of the fundamental fringe of Christianity try to force the idea of marriage upon anyone they can. And as the (currently) dominant religion of the West, this has substantial effects on how people live and what they do.[9]

It's not, of course, just Christianity that emphasises the overweening importance of this particular relationship. Marriage is a sacred imperative for religious Jews and a social imperative for non-religious Jews.[10] As anyone who's seen *Fiddler on the Roof* can confirm, the role of the matchmaker was an essential one in traditional Jewish society. Some communities still use the *shadchan*, or professional matchmaker, although more often an Orthodox couple's rabbis will have introduced them. For religious Jews marriage is a holy act, and sexuality within marriage is celebrated and welcomed as one of God's commandments. Intermarriage between a Jew and someone of another faith is frowned upon and often condemned outright, regardless of the degree of faith of the person involved. For those who live a truly religious life, the involvement of Judaism in their marriage choice and everyday life is indisputable. The religion affects every aspect of your existence, from who you spend your time with to what you eat and how you make a living. In light of this it's hardly surprising that marriage is as heavily regulated as it is. However, it's for the others, the non-observant, that this can become problematic.

Many Jews today lead secular lives, identifying themselves as a cultural or even racial group rather than as a religion. They work alongside people from all over the world, they function like them, may be indistinguishable from them, but often when it comes to the question of marriage they can face family and social pressure that's more appropriate to a more religious person. On a day-to-day level they live like anyone else, but when it comes to affairs of the heart – who to marry or even whether to marry – they suddenly feel the need to revert to more traditional type. It's a cultural dilemma that fragments people's identities, leaves them confused and floundering. How do you negotiate your way between the old and the new, the desire to be who you are and the responsibility to not turn away from your culture, when those two things turn out to be completely incompatible? Which do you walk away from, your present or your history?

Many Hindu youngsters have it just as bad, torn as they are between the desire to make their way in the 'modern' world and the need to marry someone appropriate by the appropriate age. Hinduism also has a mystical relationship to marriage, viewing it as a sacrament and not a contract.

Writing in *New York* Magazine, journalist Anita Jain discusses her parents' attempts to marry her off to a suitable boy.[11] Now 32, 'having crossed the unmarriageable threshold for an Indian woman' two years ago, Jain is well aware of the many websites out there that cater to Indians seeking an appropriate spouse – mostly because her father uses all of them to advertise her charms. She concludes that, realistically, having her dad interview prospective suitors and send them her way really isn't that much worse than any other methodology available on the New York dating scene; but consider that Jain actually *wants* to get married. Imagine how you'd feel if you didn't, but your parents were still posting your details on every available forum and searching out that elusive doctor who wouldn't mind that you were slightly over the hill.

Again, these are the consequences we face when diasporas occur, when cultures clash and young people have to negotiate their way between the one they learnt at home and the one they fit into at work.

The question of faith is, of course, essential. If you really believe that God or Allah or Buddha or, heaven forbid, L Ron Hubbard ordained a certain thing, whether that thing be the necessity of marriage or strict dietary laws, then it is not my place to criticise – and I wouldn't want to. For truly religious people who live by the tenets and laws of their books, marriage really is holy, a union blessed by God, exactly what it says on the tin during the ceremony. And respect to them. It's the rest of you I'm taking issue with, the ones who have no problem behaving in ways that would shock and appal a true believer and then scrubbing up nice and fresh to get married at an altar.

Why is it that many of us can justify sex before marriage, which is 'just a bit of fun', but not having children out of wedlock, which is 'wrong'? Is it because lots of other people will witness the children, where no one (one would hope) sees your pre-marital intercourse? If the feeling of shame likely to be evoked by irreligious behaviour is all that's stopping you, then you probably aren't pleasing God, who, after all, can see right into bedrooms and bike sheds and back seats of cars. And if it's religious leaders and nosy family members you really want to please, there's not much point dressing it up as spiritual devotion because they may not be as all-knowing and all-seeing as the Almighty and may not, thus, know exactly what's best for you.

More than these cultural perturbations, the clash between conservative religion and a more liberal environment can be devastating when it comes to parents' desires to marry off their children, more specifically their daughters. Generations of people for whom arranged marriage was an unquestionable fact of life see their newly Westernised offspring shrug off centuries of tradition, and it's hardly surprising that this can be shocking and upsetting for parents who know of no other way for their child to live a virtuous and righteous life. While an arranged marriage is a useful tool for religiously observant young people who don't get to socialise with the opposite sex, it can also be a violent, oppressive weapon used with incredible force against the unwilling.

Jasvinder Sanghera, now 41, ran away from her family home in Derby, England, when she was 15 to escape a marriage she had no interest in. Twenty-six years and much experience later she's back, but members of her family still cross the road to avoid her and she was barred from her mother's deathbed. Jasvinder runs Karma Nirvana, a chain of refuge and advice centres for South Asian women in the United Kingdom fleeing forced marriages, domestic abuse and honour killings.

The charity International Campaign Against Honour Killings defines them thus:

> These crimes occur where cultures believe that a woman's unsanctioned sexual behaviour brings such shame on the family that any female accused or suspected must be murdered. Reasons for these murders can be as trivial as talking to a man, or as innocent as suffering rape.[12]

Refusal to marry or stay with a man of the family's choice is a common cause for honour killing. We're talking about fathers murdering their own daughters because they have been raped and are now unclean, or parents forcing their children on pain of death to continue living with men who beat, rape and demean them on a daily basis. As well as being found among some Asian communities, honour killings have, according to the UN, 'been reported in Egypt, the Islamic Republic of Iran, Jordan, Lebanon, Morocco, Pakistan, the Syrian Arab Republic, Turkey, Yemen and other Mediterranean and Gulf countries, and they had also taken place in such countries as France, Germany and the United Kingdom within migrant communities'.[13]

It's pretty shocking stuff, and shockingly common. Jasvinder says:

> I get threats from men in prison saying they're going to 'sort me out'. I've had human faeces smeared all over the windows. We get 'private investigators' contacting us pretending to be sent by concerned families but who are actually bounty hunters. Awful things happen all the time: 30 per cent of those taken abroad for forced weddings are under age and I see girls who are taken to India and raped to conceive a child to make their marriage work. I worked with a girl recently who suffered

> horrific abuse with her new family and kept running home to her parents. The third time she ran home her own father stabbed her three times. In the end we had to relocate her and change her identity because the fear is always that they will seek them out.[14]

While the British government is aware of the issues of forced marriage and honour killing, Jasvinder says that they are too concerned with toeing the PC line and not offending anyone to intervene when these women's lives are at stake. The suicide rate for young Asian women is three times the UK's average; Jasvinder's own sister Robina killed herself by fire, spurring this brave woman on to face the approbation of her community and become both counsellor and campaigner.

Many forced marriages in the United Kingdom are put together with the aim of providing a UK passport for the new spouse. In this way families can pay off debts of honour or cement bonds to other families, bringing their men to England at the expense of the new wives' freedom.

Forced marriage is also said to be common in some fundamentalist Christian communities in the United States, who view pre-marital communication with the opposite sex as a sin, and insist that the word of the patriarch is absolute law and cannot be questioned. This is the darkest side of marriage for religious reasons, when it goes beyond the bounds of pressure and desire to conform and becomes abusive, destructive, inhumane.

Most of us are fortunate enough to never encounter this degree of violent fundamentalism that makes a mockery of all religious claims to care about 'the family' by ripping families apart and sacrificing them to some abstract ideal of what's appropriate. But it's worth bearing in mind that forced marriages and honour killings depend for their existence on the blind acceptance of doctrine. In most cases it's not religious law but cultural tradition accepted as holy imperative that leads to extremities of behaviour like these. And those of us who allow ourselves to be pressured into marriage to please a religious ideal we don't believe in are fostering this mindless devotion to tradition in the face of humanism, humanity, tolerance, love.

Social pressure

As if it's not bad enough having to grapple with the internalised desire to be just like everybody else, many of us also face actual bullying from our friends and family telling us how we should live our lives. Now unless your friends and family are paradigmatic examples of how to have a happy relationship and lead a satisfied life there's no reason to assume that, even if they have your best interests at heart, they know best. Their desires for you are probably filtered through all sorts of social, cultural, economic, religious and personal layers of meaning.

Perhaps they are so keen for you to get married because that's the only way you can ever reach legitimate adulthood in their version of the world. Maybe they like this boyfriend much more than the last because this one has a more respectable job, even though he isn't sure he loves you, or they want you to hurry up and have babies. Maybe they worry that you have your head in the clouds and believe getting married will bring you down to earth and make you more practical, or they don't want to lose you to a newer, shinier world that you still have the freedom to run to.

None of these caveats mean they don't love you; but they do suggest that marrying someone because the people around you think it's a good idea can be a short-cut to divorce if the people around you don't share your priorities completely.

Matilda comes from New Zealand, but she's lived all over the world. She's in her late 30s and has a son with her ex-boyfriend and an ex-husband she's still great friends with. 'I was midway through a degree and in love with a beautiful Kurdish man called Melo,' she says, 'but he was destroying me by making me work so hard in the restaurant we owned. I'd be up some stupid hour of the morning to go to flower markets and then I'd have to go to university. He was just asking too much of me.

'Then I met Aaron, who was a film maker. I was really attracted to him as a person but not as a man. He was in New Zealand doing post-production on a feature film and I started seeing him although I didn't realise he liked me in that way, and anyway I was with someone.

'Eventually we sold the restaurant and it all went to hell with Melo. Then I got a phone call from Aaron saying, why don't you come to America and work on a film with me? Seven days later I had agreed to marry him. He told me his therapist said I was the woman he was going to marry, which should have made me suspicious because he hadn't even seen his therapist in those seven days.

'I didn't know anything about Aaron, nothing. All my girl-friends in New Zealand were saying to me, "Wow, he's American and he's a film maker, you should go and be with him." I loved Melo but I listened to people who told me Aaron would be good for me.

'On my wedding day I woke up and said to Aaron, "There's something I need to tell you," and admitted I'd shagged another guy earlier that year. Then he said, "I need to talk to you about something too. There's a prenuptial I need you to sign."

'We're lying in bed and this whole thing, nine pages, got faxed through. It said he had $8 million and property worth $20 million. I had no idea at all. He's always been rather proud that I was going to marry him not for his money. I wore boots with a lacy wedding dress and I thought that was really cool, but I don't think I would have done that if I'd known I was marrying a multimillionaire.

'I didn't even know what love was when I was with Aaron. I had a comfortable friendship with him that goes on. I was very present in the marriage; in every other way we were very committed to each other. I spent eight years with him but there were large elements of being a human being that I was missing out on. I never slept around, I was never unfaithful. I denied my sexuality for eight years, I put it in a box. I didn't masturbate, nothing. We had cable that we didn't pay for – he's kind of a cheap millionaire – so we didn't have the box thing and the porn channels used to come across all scrambled. He literally spent years watching these porn channels.

'In 2002 we went to England and rented a house in Notting Hill, it was like in the movie. And then I think my sexuality just busted out. Aaron was away and I walked out of door and into the Notting Hill Carnival and there was this ocean of people, and out of the huge mass came this tall gorgeous charismatic Rasta guy and just took me around the waist and started dancing with me. That was Andre.

'So here's me, eight years married, too much money, and I kind of went mad. For about six weeks I was this rich housewife and he kept coming to visit me from the wrong side of town. I knew from the beginning that I was never going to hold him; I could have him but I couldn't hold him. I gave him the keys to the house and I went away with Aaron. I told him about Andre and we decided to have one last Christmas together.

'Andre used my house as a shag pad when I was away. I got back and there were girls' beads all over and I had to clean up from a serious orgy. But I carried on and went deeper into the relationship. Aaron, so loving – he loved me, married me and let me go. He's so magnanimous, he gave me a really generous settlement. But in the two and a half years when I was with

Andre and I was funding his nymphomania, he had about a third of that. I've quantified it during those late nights when you have nothing else to do.

'He had most of that money – but then I got my son. And weirdly, I still love Andre.'

From perfect repressed housewife to dangerously in love with the worst kind of man: that cheap wedding had unexpected knock-on effects. And then, on the flip side, there are those who manage to stave off social pressure completely, who don't want to get married at all but end up having to do so in order to continue their relationships.

Jane is in her early 60s, a British expat who lives in France with her second husband. She's a strong-minded and independent woman and doesn't give a toss about convention. Her first marriage was cut short by her husband's tragic death but both have been fundamentally good, healthy, satisfying relationships. And yet, she admits, she had no desire to marry either of them.

She says, 'There's something to me about the formal marriage, the whole thing, the big thing, that frightened me. And that was something to do with the word *wife*. I never wanted to be a wife, I wanted to be a lover. I wanted someone to be with me not because they had to. I wanted someone to choose to be with me every single day. I was always scared that once you had this ring on your finger it was inevitable that you would take somebody for granted and that the whole essence of the relationship would change.

'I got married the second time because my husband needed me to do it for tax reasons. I was quite happy the way we were, but there you go. The actual ceremony ended up being quite funny, because we were standing there – it was very small, just our kids and close family – and the registrar said, "Do you take this woman to be your lawfully wedded wife?" And I didn't mean to, I just blurted it out without thinking, "Oh please, not *wife*," really loudly. There was this long silence while the registrar stared at me in horror, then eventually he said, "Do you take this woman to be your *significant other*?" Which I was a lot happier with!

'I was also scared about getting married the first time. I had a theory that if I wasn't married I would try harder, but if I was married I'd get lazy and turn into a shrew. I wanted to be kept on my toes a little bit, I didn't want the relationship to turn into a swamp. We lived together in London, which nobody did in those days. He'd left his wife for me, but the reason we got married was because he was having trouble with his visa – he was American. I wanted a very small wedding; my father got into the act and took over and hijacked everything and made it into this big wedding.

'At the last minute I was so freaked out that I cancelled everything and I had a tiny small wedding. I had never ever visualised myself in a wedding dress, I never saw myself in something like that. I was from a relatively wealthy family, you would have expected a certain way of doing things, but I remember going to Harrods one very cold day after work. I saw this dress and tried it on over my snow boots and said it was fine, got home and thought, it's OK. Later I went to an incredibly funky hippie rock designer called Thea Porter – I paid for all this myself – and had something made. On the day of my wedding I woke up in the morning and was still deciding which one to wear. I washed my own hair. That's how fussed I was about it. I just never liked the idea of being a married couple, and if we hadn't had to do it I would not have chosen to. Either time.'

People change

One of the risks in marrying someone because it ticks the box of what you're supposed to do with your life at that stage is that he/she may seem to be looking at the same list, but you can never be sure. So you're ready to settle down, you're at the age that seems appropriate to you, marriage is the automatic Next Thing and you're raring to start adult life. How certain are you that your spouse-to-be is on the same page? How can you be sure that 'wife' and 'husband' mean the same to you both? People change after marriage; marriage changes people.

As we saw with passport marriages in Chapter Two, the cultural implications of that little piece of paper affect us all in different and sometimes crazy ways. Loose, comfortable modes of living that suited people fine when they were lovers can often seem sloppy, irresponsible and downright wrong once they get a ring on that eager little finger. Many is the man who's surprised when his Chardonnay-glugging girlfriend doesn't miraculously transform into a paragon of 'appropriate' behaviour before the tan lines from the honeymoon have faded. Many is the woman who can't understand why her new husband doesn't want her to quit her job and start incubating babies immediately.

Because we all have slightly different ideas of what marriage is, because our visions of wedded bliss are coloured by our personal stories, our histories, our childhoods, complex details we can never quite explain to our partners, the experience of getting married can be fraught with obstacles when one or both partners is or are intractable. You get married because it's 'what people do' when they reach your phase in life; but you and your partner took different paths to get to the place, no matter how similar they may look, and your paths could well diverge again. If your idea of marriage is set as an automatic event that occurs at an automatic point, you probably won't cope very well when you get into that marriage and find out that your partner has a wildly divergent view of how it's going to work.

That's what happened to Selina, 28, from South Africa. She married the appropriate boy at the appropriate time only to find out that his perception of how a woman behaves in a marriage was not one she was very keen on. She says, 'I was 27 when I got married. My ex-husband asked me to marry him after just three months of knowing me and I said yes. Everything seemed so romantic at the time, and even though I had clear signs that it was a bad idea in the eight months it took to plan the wedding I still went along with it. Looking back I feel like quite the idiot, but I figured that every couple had their problems and that we would eventually work it out. I also didn't want to go back on my decision to get married because everyone around me was so happy and excited.

'There was also an element of thinking that I was getting a bit older and that if I wanted a family and that kind of life then I should get started. I felt ready to settle down. We had the same idea (it seemed) of what marriage should be and what we wanted in life. Everything just sort of fell into place. I was happy to find someone who was serious about me and who was ready to commit. I loved the idea of him. I thought that I could overlook all the little things that niggled at the beginning, and I was very wrong.

'I come from a Christian background. So does he. I think that had a huge impact on his decision to get married. He was all for no sex before the wedding, which should have set off crazy alarm bells from the beginning. Only now do I comprehend why he wanted it that way. If anyone I date ever suggests that particular way of doing things again, I'll run a million miles. I am a Christian, but a decidedly tamer one.

'My family and friends were happy that I was happy. They all tried to get to know my soon-to-be husband, but he was quite a difficult person to get close to. The nearer we got to the wedding the more nervous everyone became. My wedding was beautiful. My mother organised most of it and it was truly a fairytale – except for marrying the wrong man, of course. My family was the highlight. I felt so much love from them and friends, and if well-wishing really worked I would have ridden into the sunset with my fricking Lancelot. I had the best of everything (paid for by my family) and I just pitched up and enjoyed it. I'm kind of spoilt, but I really did appreciate my family's love and sweat that went into the wedding.'

Despite getting off to a great start, Selina's marriage began to show strain from the outset. 'We started fighting right away on the honeymoon. He became very demanding and very specific about what he did and didn't want. Everything had to be done his way. He wanted me to start working harder. I had a full-time job, but he expected me to start another business so I could pay off the house quicker. He became critical of my weight and appearance, and he made me read relationship self-help books. According to him I was very selfish. He also started travelling with work extensively. He would sometimes be away for two weeks out of a month. This continued throughout the seven months we were together, and just got more and more.

'I am very liberal and he put up a façade of being that too. After the marriage, however, I feel like he expected me to crochet him some nifty hankies while juggling my job and my new venture. He wanted me to have the meals ready, the house and dogs taken care of as well as pay the house bond and a lot of the month's expenses. Needless to say, I am not an idiot and as soon as I realised what he was trying to turn me into, we started having heavy rows and consequently got divorced. I tried my best. I just feel that my talents are better utilised out in the big bad world. As much as I would love to sit in the back yard and shake a jar of cream until it turns to butter, I didn't go and get an education so I could appease a fool by not thinking for myself. I am who I am, and he knew that before we got married. It worked for him then. What changed?

'The actual divorce was much more pleasant than the marriage. I think both of us just wanted it done as soon as possible, and that meant we had to play nice. I've never really seen us work together so nicely. It was like taking off a tight shoe that hurt. My uncle was my lawyer and everything went smoothly. I was a little embarrassed, but I figure people will forget in a couple of years. Not that I really care. We were married for such a short amount of time that there weren't too many complications. The faster the better – it's like pulling off a plaster.

'I don't know if I'd get married again. Maybe, but it would take a long time for me to make that commitment again. I would have to be completely sure of my story. I have to say it's not probable in the near future.'

A dramatic turnaround, but a lesson well learned. Doing the expected thing, doing what everyone else is doing, shutting your eyes and following the herd and hoping for the best, is a slippery slope that can send you careering off in the opposite direction from the one you thought you wanted.

Chapter Five

'We wanted to have kids'

'I believe,' sang the inimitable Whitney Houston in her 1986 hit 'Greatest love of all', 'the children are our future.' As do many of us. And many of us, despite adoring kids and being full of the desire to be parents, don't meet the right person to be one with. Or don't meet the right person soon enough. Or meet the right person two years before they come out of the closet.

So there you are, a woman, or increasingly frequently a man as social changes make single fatherhood more acceptable, who has a huge pile of unclaimed love and nary an adorable tot to shower it on. Should you be prevented from becoming a parent by this unhappy accident of fate? Leaving aside questions of over-population, the disproportionately huge amount of natural resources utilised by your average first-world individual and the consequent ethics of having children at all, there are many people out there who would make excellent, loving, supportive and nurturing mums and dads but who aren't lucky enough to find the perfect person to co-parent with. Which means they have three choices: give it up, go it alone or attach yourself to someone you don't want to be with for 20-odd years and see how happy *that* makes you.

Before the moral majority start camping outside my house with their rusty lynching equipment, I'd like to make it clear that I'm perfectly aware that having two parents is far better for kids than having one. As the child of a divorced couple I know I suffered in certain ways without my father's day-to-day presence, and I know the burden on my mother to raise two kids alone was pretty overwhelming at times. But would I rather not have been born? I don't think so. And would my mother rather not have had us than have had to bring us up by herself? I bloody hope not. (Mum, if you're reading this, the correct response is, 'It was worth every second.')

It is unquestionably the ideal situation when two people who care about each other come together to raise children with whom they share that care, but the world we live in is far from ideal and life gets messy. That's just how it is. So bearing that in mind, perhaps we can have a clearer look at the complex art of child-rearing without the blinkers imposed by the monotheistic religious idealism or unbending conservative traditionalism that insist unless you've hoppity-skipped it down an aisle in a meringue or a monkey suit you're not fit to be the moral guardian of a young mind.

I am not advocating that everyone who wants to have a child should just go out and get one by whatever means necessary, disregarding entirely the premise of two parents for one kid. What I am suggesting, though, is that wanting children is not necessarily a good enough reason to get married unless you're damn sure the marriage would work anyway. A bad marriage can be just as destructive for children as no marriage at all, and significantly more so in some cases. Kids need happy parents; attaching yourself to someone for life just because they managed to impregnate you or you managed to impregnate them does not make for a loving home or a stable environment for your children.

As we saw in Chapter One, the hormones and chemicals that regulate love do not last very long. Those that regulate sex are even more transient, and sex, as I hope we all know by now, is what leads to babies. Which means that just because you want to sleep with someone, just because a happy accident of their pheromones and facial DNA creates a physical attraction between you, does not mean that you want to spend a huge amount of time with them doing deeply unsexy things like changing nappies, dealing with cracked nipples and suffering extreme sleep deprivation. Sex is fun (unless you're doing it wrong, in which case you're reading the wrong book) but children, while they can be fun too, are above all else a serious business. And like any serious business parenthood should not entered into lightly, and nor should the idea of partnership, of doing all this serious stuff with someone else.

Famous families: a variety show

There is a whole host of possibilities that presents itself around the issue of raising kids. Like most things in life there's not just one way to do it, although it would be easy to believe that considering how often single parents are demonised. Let's take yet another peek at our impeccable gauge of modern life, the ker-azy world of celebrities. Having a child was once considered career suicide for an actress. Back in 1935 Loretta Young faked the adoption of her own daughter by Clark Gable because she was so afraid of admitting to being her biological mother, even going so far as to alter the girl's face with plastic surgery when her celebrity parentage threatened to become obvious.

But these days motherhood is not only acceptable, it's expected – in all sorts of permutations. Angelina Jolie adopted her Cambodian son Maddox before she and Brad Pitt rocked modern civilisation by becoming the Best Looking Couple

Ever™. She then adopted a daughter from Ethiopia, gave birth to their biological daughter and adopted a son from Vietnam. And that's just at the time of writing – I expect that when this book is published she'll also have a pair of twins from Peru and a few Albanian refugees. Calista Flockhart had adopted baby Liam before she shacked up with her ageing action hero Harrison Ford. Madonna, back in the day when she was livin' on the edge, got herself knocked up by personal trainer Carlos Leon because he had the best genes she could find. The result, daughter Lourdes, was very much her child, although she's now being raised in a nice nuclear family along with the singer and her husband's biological and adopted sons. What all this is getting at is that there are many ways to skin a cat (although people who habitually skin cats should probably not be allowed to have children).

There's no question that those genetically superior few who live their lives in the hallowed halls of Hollywood have options that don't apply to the rest of us and a degree of financial freedom that we can never dream of. But nonetheless the fact that the famous are having their kids in so many varied ways bodes nothing but good for 'civilians'. If the primary reason for having children only within a marriage, no matter how miserable, was to save them from being ostracised or punished, it's no longer a problem. Which means we can make our choices based on more sensible, sober reasons, like what we really want, and what will make everyone happiest, and what our horoscopes suggest.

Perhaps you can't provide your potential children with a station wagon, a Labrador and 2.4 television sets; you may have something to give them that's a lot more valuable, even if it's a lot less common. And more and more of us are beginning to realise this. According to the UK's Office for National Statistics, children are three times more likely to live in one-parent households than they were in 1972. Since 1971 the proportion of people living in 'traditional' family households of married couples with dependent children has fallen from 52 per cent to 37 per cent. Nearly a quarter of children lived with only one parent in 2006, and nine out of ten of those households were headed by lone mothers.[1] The stigma is fading, and with it the need to remain in unhappy situations.

Sometimes selfishness helps

All too often people get married because there's been an accidental pregnancy or because they can't see another way to have children. And what happens once you're stuck in a marriage that makes you miserable? Do you bite the bullet and give up on any idea of personal happiness, or do you do the dastardly deed and contemplate divorce, even if it could 'ruin your children's lives'? Divorce is generally a pretty traumatic experience for kids, but so is living in a house with parents who fight all the time.

There are no statistics that prove whether two parents and a horrible home life or an eventual messy divorce is more or less damaging for kids than one happy functional parent, but I would venture to suggest that the latter is the preferable situation. And here's where it gets a bit non-PC. Our society insists blindly, vehemently, on the primacy of children. There are unspoken laws that state that as soon you become a parent self-interest flies out the window and you turn into a walking paragon of sacrifice. I dispute this assumption for a number of reasons, not the least being that having kids in the first place is a pretty selfish act that people commit because they *want* children. Adopting, now *that's* selfless and noble. Having your own when there are so many out there in need? Self-interest, the desire to see your own genes reflected in someone else's face.

Unless you're extremely religious (in which case why were you having sex when you didn't want kids?) or your partner in crime is a controlling psychopath, no one's actively forcing you to have children. The souls of your unborn babes aren't flying around your head begging to be born and pleading with you to stop being so darned selfish and get on with turning yourself into a model of parental virtue. (If they are, I'm afraid I can't help you and you might require something stronger than literature.) Contraception is freely available across the developed world, and if you choose not to take advantage of that option, you can't realistically go claiming ignorance.[2] You have kids because you want to. Or because it just happened. Or because it was the obvious step to take. But at the end of the day it's all about you, and there's nothing unselfish about that. I don't say this in a critical way; contrary to popular belief there is nothing wrong with self-interest. It's the Homo sapien's way.

We all take care of ourselves first, and even our altruism is often geared towards making us feel better about ourselves. Plagued with guilt about starving children in Africa? Give some money to Oxfam every month and feel better. *Truly* unselfish would be to sell your home and car and go out there to work in a refugee camp. But we don't do this and we're not expected to, by ourselves or by our societies. Self-interest only becomes problematic, as far as I can see, when it gets wildly out of hand or masquerades as selflessness.

The very fact that people will make uncharacteristic sacrifices, including betraying principles they've always held dear, so their own children get a leg up over all the other children in the world does put something of a damper on the idea that popping out a baby makes you into a saint. You become altruistic and selfless only in the cause of advancing your own offspring, who you had for your own purposes anyway. It may be different from the way we normally carry on but it can't be equated with genuine selflessness. We have children because it will make us happy. So if we can put the kibosh on that particular social myth, maybe then we can examine the fact that some of the demands made on parents are both unrealistic and unfair.

Back in days of yore children were expected to go out to work, or at least to help with the family industry as soon as they were capable: working in a shop, tilling the fields, looking after livestock or helping to run the home. Families often lived in more extended groupings than we're used to today, which meant that children would be involved in caring for their aged parents in practical ways. Today you're lucky if your kids look after you financially. So all of these sacrifices that you're supposed to make come only with an emotional pay-off – which can, I don't doubt, make it all worthwhile.

But what happens when you marry someone because one of you is pregnant or because you want to have children, and then in 20 years those children leave home? What's happened to your life then? What's left for you? And it's here that I'm advocating selfishness, as much as we can manage. Look after yourself *as well as* your children, live a life that makes you happy. Martyrdom is not a good look for anyone.

And even this is not as selfish as it sounds. Children learn by example. No matter how many lovely things you say to them and how much you pretend that everything's hunky dory, if you are really unhappy *they will know*. And happy people make much, much better parents. Some relationships are such that the participants can be fairly content living their lives together even if it's hardly fireworks and romance, but some are horrible. Some wreck lives, especially when the people involved are clinging onto the last vestiges of something they only imagined they had together, spending their days swimming through a swamp of mutual antipathy that they think it's their duty to put up with 'for the sake of the children'.

And those children? What will they learn about relationships at their parents' knees? If they follow the pattern they were taught by Mum and Dad, a very common occurrence, they may one day grow up to have shitty relationships that they stay in unhappily for the sake of their own children. Surely this is not a healthy cycle to be repeating. Staying together for the kids may be the noble, self-sacrificing option, and yes, two parents in one home is the optimal situation, but sometimes children would be better off if their parents weren't so damn unhappy.

Jean, 31, is an only child and a writer. She's bright, productive, confident, beautiful, all the things you'd expect from an intelligent, well-educated 21st-century woman. But she's convinced that she could have been very different if her parents' marriage hadn't ended when it did – and this despite the fact that her mother only stayed in it for her sake.

'My mum got married in her early 20s but sadly had bad taste in men,' she says. 'Although my father was good in some ways – teaching me how to read before I went to school, and spending hours talking to me – once he had a few drinks inside him, he changed totally. He became very aggressive and violent towards both me and my mother. We'd lock ourselves in the bathroom – the only room in the house with a lock – every Friday night when he went to the pub because otherwise we'd get hit when he got back. My earliest memory of him is having a play fight when I accidentally stood on his foot, so he hit me full fist in the face. I was four. He'd also psychologically torture me – make me eat things I didn't want to, like snails, and not French snails out of a tin. He'd throw garden snails on a bonfire then scoop them out and make me eat them, saying that they ate snails in France and I shouldn't be so silly.

'Eventually, when I was seven, he beat my mum so badly that she was worried he'd kill her. That night we ran away, and she divorced him later that year. I wish she'd divorced him years before – but she said to me when I was older that she didn't want to disrupt my life and thought it was best to stay with him for my sake. In a way, I'm glad things got so extreme that she left because otherwise I'd have spent my whole childhood growing up scared and I'm sure I'd be a very different – very damaged – person now.'

Not all bad marriages involve abuse, and anyone experiencing this kind of treatment from their partner should run away as fast as their poor bruised legs can carry them. But the fact that Jean's mother was willing to stay with her father until the situation got as out of control as it did is a testament to how strong the prohibition is against leaving a marriage when you have children. To take that level of abuse in the mistaken belief that having two parents around is better than having one may seem insane to the casual observer, but such is the nature of the twin social obsessions with the importance of putting children first and the unshakeable significance of the nuclear family grouping. Jean herself, meanwhile, is a testament to just how well you can turn out when you're raised by only one parent.

Children and divorce

I can't pretend the statistics don't prove that divorce is self-perpetuating, that children of broken homes aren't more likely to get divorced themselves. As of 1995 in the United States, 43 per cent of women with divorced parents ended their own marriages within ten years compared with 29 per cent of women whose parents stayed together. In 1996 children of divorced parents were 50 per cent more likely to go through a divorce themselves.[3] This is an unpalatable fact that could easily influence a parent's decision on what to do about an unhappy marriage.

What we don't know, though, is how many children grow up to remain in bad relationships because they witnessed their folks doing it, and what kind of effect that has on their lives. This sort of consequence is a lot less easy to quantify mathematically and is of far less interest to the government social scientists who usually conduct such research, so it's hardly surprising that figures aren't forthcoming.[4] If there were a way to measure it, though, I'd put money on the fact that being the child of a miserable couple who despise each other can be just as damaging, just as cyclical, as being the child of a divorced couple. Which is worse? We'll never know, and there tends to not be an optimal option in sad situations like these.[5] What it does mean, though, is that as a parent you have some degree of choice. Leaving a bad marriage is *not* equivalent to betraying your children, no matter how much guilt you might feel.

Christine Northam, of the UK's family counselling service Relate, says:

> The parents' marriage is hugely influential. It's statistically proven that if your parents divorced then you're more likely to, but the children of divorced parents have also seen it happen before so sometimes they're more determined to make their marriages work, and often they'll be quick to seek counselling. But also, those people know that it's not the end of the world and that you can come out the other side of a divorce okay. A US study showed that people who survived their parents' divorces okay became more resilient. Relate always make a splitting couple aware of what their divorce is doing to their kids. We take it very seriously; it's well documented how much it affects kids. There are studies proven where the children say they'd rather their parents had stayed together no matter how miserable they were, but then others

> where the kids say they wanted their parents to be happy so the split was a really good idea. It's completely subjective depending on who you listen to.[6]

Divorce is never ideal and it has painful after-effects.[7] Of course it's never a decision to be taken lightly. Avoiding the necessity for divorce would far and away be the best life strategy, but staying in a toxic, suffocating marriage is not a good idea either, for oneself or for one's children.

According to a recent study, the most ambitious ever undertaken on the issue, people who get divorced never really regain the state of happiness they had before it happened. Richard Lucas, from Michigan State University and the German Institute of Economic Research, followed over 30,000 people for 18 years to complete these findings. He says, 'One of the most surprising findings in the study was that divorce was associated with permanent changes in levels of distress.' However, it's not as cut and dried as all that. There are more things to be learnt from this study than the obvious. Lucas reported seeing a marked decrease in his subjects' levels of happiness all across the years leading up to the divorce.[8]

Divorce may be the lowest point, but it's being in a bad marriage that makes people miserable. A 1997 study, led by Kathleen Kiernan and published by the Centre for the Analysis of Social Exclusion (CASE) at the London School of Economics, suggests that financial hardship and other factors that come before a divorce can have just as much negative effect on children as the traumatic event itself, and could go a long way to explaining why the children of single parents statistically seem to face more difficulties in their adult lives.[9] Children of parents who stayed together seem on average to have better qualifications and find better jobs, but Kiernan's work suggests this is largely down to their families being in a more favourable social position to start with, with more money and education giving them a better start in life.

The research used data from the UK's National Child Development Study, which has followed the lives of more than 11,400 children born in 1958, and came to the conclusion that the children's experience of divorce was actually not the main reason for some adult differences between them and their peers. While a greater percentage of children from divorced parents lacked qualifications by the time they were 33, financial trouble and behavioural problems were largely to blame. Male children of divorced parents are more like to experience unemployment, but again, the research showed that financial trouble before their parents' break-up was responsible for this, and factoring in the divorce made little difference to the numbers. The same is true of adults who live in council housing – divorce may have been a common factor but early poverty was far more significantly responsible, and again the fact of divorce barely altered the odds. Dr Kiernan explains:

> Although children from divorced families tend to have more negative experiences than those reared by both parents, their qualifications and economic circumstances appear to be heavily influenced by factors at work before the break-up. Undoubtedly, children benefit from being raised in a secure two-parent family. But if that is not possible, then the evidence from this study suggests that those concerned with children's long-term welfare should attend to financial hardship and other conditions that precede family breakdown as well as to its legacy.[10]

In their book *Freakonomics: A Rogue Economist Explores the Hidden Side of Everything,*[11] Steven Levitt and Stephen Dubner used data from the US Department of Education's enormous Early Childhood Longitudinal Study, which measured the progress of more than 20,000 US children in the late 1990s to prove some startling facts. They isolated various factors that had a strong correlation with children's improved test scores and others that didn't, and then paired them up. It turned out that once racial, gender and socio-economic factors had been taken into account, having an intact two-parent family actually did not impact on children's success at school. They write:

> Whether a child's family is intact doesn't seem to matter. Just as the earlier-cited studies show that family structure has little impact on a child's personality, it does not seem to affect his academic ability either. This is not to say that families ought to go around splitting up willy-nilly. It should, however, offer encouragement to the roughly twenty million American schoolchildren being raised by a single parent.

What all of this goes to show is that as unpleasant as it may be, divorce itself is not the bad guy. If our governments were altruistically concerned with the welfare of children in the lower strata of society (rather than just being censorious and bossy and prescriptive) they would help families out economically, provide them with better healthcare and education, rather than waiting for the parents to split up and then waggling their fingers delightedly and bemoaning the irresponsibility of the lower classes.

A poll conducted by InsideDivorce.com and published in the UK *Guardian* in January 2007 interviewed 341 children whose parents had been through a divorce.[12] The researchers found that 80 per cent of these children said their home life was the same or better after divorce, and only a quarter wanted their parents to get back together. The children said the biggest benefit of divorce was an end to arguments, while the worst drawback was parents bickering over the time they got to spend with them.

Andrew is 11 years old and was just two when his parents split up. He and his brother Stefan are absolutely unshakeable in their conviction that life is better now than it was then, agreeing that the end of arguments is the best thing about the divorce. They live with their mother and see their father on alternate weekends, sharing school holidays between the two. Andrew says, 'I remember being sad when Mum told me Dad had moved somewhere else. But we see lots of both of them now, and they don't argue any more and Dad lives near by.' Nine-year-old Stefan says, 'Mum and Dad are both lots of fun. Sometimes when me and my brother are having fun with Dad I feel sad that Mum isn't there to join in.' Their mother Gennifer, 45, credits the lack of bitterness and good communication she has with her ex-husband with the boys' contentment. 'What's important is agreeing how we bring the boys up,' she says.

Amy is in her late 40s and believes she and her ex have done a perfectly good job of raising their kids, despite divorcing years ago. 'As a divorcee with two almost adult sons who have done well at school and seem to be well adjusted, I firmly believe that a happy single-parent family is preferable to an unhappy two-parent family,' she says. 'My sons continue to see their father (after 13 years living with their mother). Financially we have been reasonably secure but not well off. I believe these last two factors are the most relevant issues. Better to have a happy mother, contact with their father and reduced but manageable financial circumstances than two unhappy parents forced to stay together for financial reasons and taking out their frustrations within the "family unit".'

These are the good examples of the lucky families; having an easy and amicable divorce depends very much on personality, financial status and the circumstances of the split. But not getting divorced because you're likely to have a tough one implies that your marriage must be in fairly dire straits already, which really isn't a good reason for continuing it.

All of that said, divorce really shouldn't be the issue when it comes to children. Whatever state their parents' relationship is in, children should come first. But too often they don't and those oversights can't be blamed on the relative ease of dissolving a legal partnership. Whether you've been married and raising a family for ten years or decided to have the child of a casual affair, your responsibilities to that little person are identical. You cannot divorce your children; married or not, you have a moral, spiritual and financial imperative to stick by them until they don't need you any more.

All the focus on marriage and divorce tends to muddy the waters; you can be a terrible parent in any relationship, and having a ring on your finger doesn't make you any more mature or caring or responsible. In fact it can sometimes do just the opposite; what does marriage mean but that you've hitched your wagon to another adult? And if their primary purpose in your life is as personal partner rather than co-parent it doesn't take a genius to spot how easily things can go wrong as far as the kids are concerned. When couples focus so intensely on their over-the-top wedding days and the perfect marriages they believe they're entitled to, children can be downgraded into accessories to that TV fantasy, battered about by the dramas of their parents' lives. All the emphasis on marriage actually serves to lessen the importance of the far more crucial role of parenting.

UK psychotherapist Phillip Hodson says:

> What we need is a philosophy that says that however you partner doesn't matter – what matters is how you parent. Children are far and away the most important thing, and more of a public issue than marriage. Who you share your bed with can and should remain a private concern; the government has no

need to legislate your sleeping arrangements because they affect no one but you. But when children are abandoned and neglected the state, which means the taxpayer, shoulders the burden. So society has every right to get involved. No child asks to be born, and you have a duty of care to your offspring, far more than if you make a series of promises to a lover. People tend to emphasise the marital day as the most important of their lives, but that's flawed reasoning; the natal day is far more crucial with far longer-reaching repercussions.

I find it scandalous that we make so much relative fuss about the scale of adultery while remaining utterly blasé when parents enter a second union before they've finished looking after the children from the first. All the emphasis in our legislative and tax system, as well as the organisation of private ceremonies, should be poured into this single, defining moment. The state should be preoccupied with parenting, not partnering. The vital question for any responsible adult is mating, not marriage.[13]

Francesca is in her early 30s. She lives in London and works in the media. She's smart and independent and not the kind of woman you'd imagine would be coerced into anything, but when she unexpectedly got pregnant she found herself pressured into marriage.

She explains, 'I got married when I was 25. It's not that young but it's not that old either. I was about five months pregnant. It's not that I minded having a child out of wedlock – he did, and my mum did, and his mum did, so suddenly I had about 20 people shouting at me to get married. I knew I didn't want to but eventually I started to think, well, everybody else must know what they're talking about and I'm just being headstrong.

'There was no space to renegotiate anything in the relationship, which is what happens when you get married in a hurry – certain things get set quite quickly. If you're pregnant you're going to end up at home doing the mothering. You don't have a place in the marriage as a working woman, you're going to spend the next year at home doing childcare regardless of what you want.'

Rather than marrying a long-term boyfriend or someone she was stupidly in love with, Francesca found herself in the unenviable position of having a husband she wasn't entirely sure about.

'We'd been together six months when I got pregnant. It was a year till we got married. It was definitely an unlikely relationship but I was really prepared to give it a go. I still like this man and I wonder sometimes whether it would have worked out if circumstances had been different.

'For about three years of the marriage I was quite determined not to get out of it. I thought, I've married this guy, that's it, that's fine. It was a belief in marriage and also the fact that we do really get on. I thought it was salvageable, I convinced myself that our problems were just me in my mid-20s being "difficult". I retreated into myself and into my kitchen. I started doing this thing my friends call compensation cooking, when you don't love somebody enough so you start cooking them marvellous meals. Then I'd go upstairs and play computer games till four in the morning so I wouldn't have to go to bed at the same time as him and he couldn't pester me for sex.

'We would go for a month without talking to each other, just yes and no. I would have these last-ditch discussions where I'd explain how unhappy I was and how my career was going nowhere and blah blah blah. I'd be in floods of tears at the kitchen table and he'd just sit there and say, "But I love you and I just try to do my best."

'It took quite a long time to admit that I was going to leave. I almost told him the day before my 29th birthday but I chickened out, then I started having an affair a few months after that. I was working full time and having this affair so he basically never saw me. I wasn't there. Then I finished the affair and my job finished, and I thought, bugger it, those two have gone, might as well get rid of the third.

'So I told him the marriage had nowhere to go, and he suddenly perked up and went to counselling. I agreed to go too, but when we got there I said to him, "Look, I don't want to get back together. Let's talk about how to do a mediated split. The moment has passed, I'm sorry." I'd had so much therapy that I hadn't got years worth of resentment towards him. That was part of the reason our divorce went well. He'd get into a tantrum, but rather than rising to it I'd let it wash over me. I think most people who split up aren't in that position.'

Caught up as she was with wading through her unhappiness and her husband's incomprehension, Francesca had let another hugely important part of her life slip to the point where it required serious rescuing.

'I had a pretty rocky relationship with my daughter up to this point, but the main reason for that was because I had such a bad relationship with him,' she says. 'He's a great dad, he still has her three times a week and is very involved. There was a point in the divorce where he was talking about having full custody, which I was livid about. Because I was failing as a mother in his eyes he'd take over the parenting and be quite aggressive about it, which made me feel like shit. He attacked my mothering. There was a point when, in theory, he could have taken custody, but for some reason I dug my heels in and said she's my daughter and she's staying with me. When he left I had to really patch up my relationship with her, I had to start being a parent. Up till then I'd been too busy being miserable.'

Other ways to be a parent

If we've managed to dispel the spectre of divorce somewhat, then what other options are left for prospective parents who aren't part of a nice normal nuclear white-bread mum-and-pop family? The list may not be endless but it's pretty damn long. All sorts of people can raise children effectively in all sorts of environments. Recent figures paint a surprising picture of the make-up of family life in the United States.[14]

Single parents account for 27 per cent of family households with children under 18. More than 2 million fathers are the primary caregivers of children under 18, a 62 per cent increase since 1990. One in two US children will live in a single-parent family at some point in childhood. One out of every three children is born to unmarried parents. Between 1978 and 1996, the number of babies born to unmarried women per year quadrupled from 500,000 to more than 2 million. The number of single mothers increased from 3 million to 10 million between 1970 and 2000. More than half of US citizens today have been, are or will be in one or more step-family situations.

One child out of 25 lives with neither parent. The 2000 US Census found that 2.4 million grandparents are the primary caregivers for the children in their families. In 1996, more than 5.2 million children lived with one biological parent and either a step-parent or adoptive parent, up from 4.5 million in 1991. The 2000 Census showed that 2.8 million children under the age of 18 and nearly 7 million US citizens of all ages identify with more than one race. Approximately 2 million US children under the age of 18 are being raised by lesbian or gay parents. One-third of lesbian households and one-fifth of gay male households have children. The UK's Office of National Statistics estimates that there are 1.69 million lone UK parents with dependent children.[15] In Sweden and Denmark, about 80 per cent of lone parents are in full-time jobs.

Same-sex parents, working mothers, interracial families, single mums and dads, babies born out of wedlock: to a preacher from the 1950s it would sound like the kind of nightmare you get from indulging in cannabis and heavy petting, but to me it sounds a lot like emancipation, like people making choices that work for them and having the kind of lives and families they feel comfortable with. Sure, a lot of the single parents may have been pushed into their situations by circumstance, but that doesn't mean they're not doing really good jobs despite the conventional belief that certain people 'aren't fit' to raise children.

A lot of these new types of families may have consciously chosen to live the way they do. Like the celebrity variations we looked at earlier, these many types of families point to a sweeping social change. No matter what the policymakers think about it, no matter how religious leaders try to paint it as the breakdown of civilisation as we know it, the married nuclear family – which as we now know is a fairly recent invention anyway – is no longer the only model for child rearing. It may be dominant but that doesn't mean you have to do it.

Illegitimacy is no longer a crime; you do not, in most of Western Europe and North America, have to be married to grant your children respectability. Whether you raise them alone or as a couple or in a commune where everyone eats lentils and weaves their own sandals out of quinoa, you can be a loving and effective parent without knotting yourself up in a marriage you don't want to be in. Now that's nothing if not liberating. And if the statistics still suggest that two-parent children have a much better time of it, the statistics are going to have to do some catching up: maybe not yet, but soon, as the trends of human society diversify and more and types and families become more and more common. But let's let a few of the single parents speak for themselves.

Luella is 34. She has a 12-year-old daughter she's raised more or less alone, and is now pregnant with her new partner's baby. She admits to being slightly unsure about how to raise a child with someone else – and she thinks that her being a single mum has given her daughter some distinct advantages that she can see other children have missed, as well as the more obvious disadvantages.

She says, 'There's no being undermined or playing one parent off against the other if it's just you, so your kid takes you seriously and listens to you, and that teaches them a lot of respect. Your child is more sensitive if there's only you and them – at least mine is. They're less likely to be a brattish alpha kid as they know they're number one and don't have to prove it; and they're less devious, less aggressive, more honest, kinder, gentler. They have to take more responsibility for themselves and they learn to be wise in different ways to other kids.

'We spend a lot of time with my friends who have children the same age as mine; my daughter is frequently gobsmacked at the way some of the kids speak to their mums and dads. I think this is because they see their dads and mums interact in a shitty way – which we all do from time to time – and they don't learn that it's inappropriate.

'My daughter is a complete joy, I don't think she could have turned out better. And that's not because I'm such an amazing mother, it's because of a combination of circumstance and her character. There are downsides of course. They seldom see conflicts resolved so they're not that good at the "you can apologise and move on from this" ability. It's always your turn to do everything, whether that's running her bath, ironing her uniform, taking her for shoes, whatever. You have to make the big decisions (like I did with school) – nobody else cares as much as you do about what happens to them, big decisions are hard to take although you just have to stand by them. And there's nobody going, "I *told* you that was wrong." So yeah, not always easy. But kids are exhausting anyway, no matter how you have them.'

Najma is 28. She never expected to be a single parent but made the decision to go it alone after her marriage became intolerable and she realised her son would be better off alone with her.

'I met my husband while we were in high school and it all felt like a sweet dream. High school sweethearts, you know? I married him when I turned 18, two years after we met. From the beginning I wanted a child so badly it hurt. My husband, at first, was a sweet, romantic and loving man. I never thought that I could live without him, never thought our marriage was going to end.

'About a year and a half into our marriage we finally conceived. It was great – everything I ever thought it would be. At the time we thought it would be a good idea to move in with his mother. But during my pregnancy I realised the man I had loved for all these years was revealing his true colours. His mother and him would make comments like, "It better be a boy or we'll give her up for adoption." Being pregnant and not knowing the sex of my child, this would often get me upset. My supportive husband was no longer there. Instead, a man stood before me with an evil grin. Call this mental abuse, psychological abuse, whatever. I knew one thing – I was no longer happy with him.

'Once my son was born (oh, they were happy about that!) things got even worse. He would criticise every aspect of my mothering, starting with breastfeeding, co-sleeping, and every other decision I made concerning my newborn son. But at the same time he would never spend any time alone with our boy, and when he did it would be for ten minutes – not even long enough for me to shower without worrying. When my son turned nine months old my mother-in-law wanted to take him on a "vacation" to another country, but said I couldn't join them (my husband was also going). When I refused, fearing I would never see my child again, they threatened to get custody. At this point I knew that if I wanted my son to be happy and safe, I had to leave. Ten months later and here I am. Motherhood has blessed me. I am stronger than I ever thought I would be, happier than ever before, and safer.

'I do feel guilty for my son growing up without a father. His father has lost his supervised visitation rights, has not paid any of the court-ordered child support and has been trying to play games with me ever since we separated. But I do regret my son not having a strong male role model around.

'When I left his father and went to court to get custody, the judge asked me what I do. It felt like the whole scene had frozen, and I was thinking, "What do you mean what do I do? I'm a mom! Believe it or not, that's more than any full-time position. You don't even get a lunch break!" Then I heard her ask, "Do you work? Do you go to school?" And I sadly thought, "No, I don't go to school, I wish I had." But I heard myself saying, "Yes, I'm starting school this September." My head was yelling at me, "What are you doing? You don't go to school," but I answered right back, "I guess I do!" So before I knew it, September came around and I was enrolled.

'My first semester has just ended. I'm majoring in paralegal (always good to know the laws!) and have been loving it. I'm getting excellent grades and it's comforting to know that my son is close by in campus day care. I know that he's safe, happy, and interacting with other children. And I made that happen by myself.'

It isn't just women who are pulling it all together when their relationships don't work out. Single fathers are on the increase too, and despite the mass assumption that women have an innate parenting ability that men lack, they're doing just fine at it. A US-wide study published at the end of the 1990s by researchers at Ohio State University questioned the validity of the widely held belief that mothers are better positioned to be primary caregivers, and the contrasting idea that children who grow up without fathers are innately disadvantaged.[16] In a comparison of 456 15- and 16-year-olds who lived in single-father households and 2,583 teens who lived in single-mother households, both groups were remarkably similar in terms of behaviour, relationships and school performance, once factors such as family income and parent education were accounted for.

According to Douglas Downey, sociology professor and co-author of the study:

> It's well known that there are a lot of problems associated with children who grow up in single-mother households. But our results suggest the problems aren't mainly due to the lack of a father. We believe the problems rise more from the fact that single mothers are more likely to be disadvantaged in terms of income and other factors.

Researchers have long assumed that because men generally score better on quantitative skills children raised by their father would do well at maths, while children raised by women, who generally score better at verbal tests, would be better at English. But the Ohio State study proved this as a myth; there was no discernible difference in the children's skills. In fact, Downey says, the biggest differences they found were influenced by the economic backgrounds of the children. 'For nearly every demographic and background characteristic that we measured, single mothers were disadvantaged compared with single fathers,' he explains. 'People have assumed that the sex of the parent has a major effect on children's development, but we found that isn't the case. Researchers need to focus on other factors, such as family resources, which seem to have a real impact.'

With divorce, the years leading up to the event are a large part of the trauma that affects children; with single parenting, the economic background of the parent is a major factor. So it's about more than the scare stories of how we'll mess up our kids – it's about where we come from, and, like most things, how much financial security and education we have.

Seth's story is a real heart-warmer. Twenty-eight, single and not physically capable of fathering, he has no children but has always wanted them. Unlike the many women who find themselves in this position and have the option of just getting pregnant, Seth's having to find entirely new ways around the problem. And he's being pretty creative about it.

He says, 'I'm a fairly average guy. I'm working toward my Masters in library science while working in the field. In my spare time I kayak, try to find people to rock climb with, fool around with my dog and tinker with an old bike. The main thing about me is that I'm in the process of getting certified as a foster parent, with the intent to adopt once I finish school in about a year and a half. I've wanted to be a parent all my life, and I'm not able to be a biological father due to a medical condition. I've been single for a couple of years and I'm coming up on 30 so I finally decided I should quit holding my breath for the right girl to come along and go ahead and start building a family on my own.

'I know I can't commit to full-time parenting as long as I'm in school, so I'll be providing short-term foster/respite care. I'm not sure at this point whether I'll adopt from within the system or pursue independent adoption; a lot of that will depend on finances. I feel that adopting a same-race infant might minimise my challenges for the first go-round, but eventually I'd like to adopt older kids, kids with disabilities, sibling groups, and/or kids of colour (I'm white). I feel really positive about this but also a little anxious. It's scary to think about doing this without the built-in support of a partner or spouse, and I keep waking up thinking, "Oh, man, car seats! They grow out of those!".

'I'm confident about my ability to care for children – I've been taking care of kids since I was nine years old, and spent a year and a half as a full-time nanny a few years ago – but I know it's hard to prepare for the realities of parenthood, especially as a single parent and maybe even more so as a single dad. But I think I'm ready.'

Single parenting may not be easy, especially for those who are forced into this position and have to deal with the break-up of a relationship too, but it's possible, and it brings its own unique rewards. Would Najma have been any happier if she'd stayed with her husband? Unlikely. And despite the guilt she feels about her son not having his dad around, she knows from bitter experience that this is the healthiest way for him to grow up.

Najma and Luella are in very different positions; one found that her fairytale romance was actually a psychotic nightmare, while the other had a manageable relationship with her ex and no broken dreams left in his wake. Bringing up a child alone is always going to be easier if you don't enter into it thinking that you'll sail through the rest of your life with your perfect partner by your side, only to find that they've sprouted wings and soared elsewhere, or grown an extra head and become monstrous. No one's saying it's an ideal position, and Lord knows single parents – especially mothers – get more than their fair share of bad press. But it can be done, is done, every day, by brave and tough men and women who are making this way of parenting more acceptable and more workable.

And alongside the single parents are the committed couples who happily have their kids without feeling the need to get married as soon as the baby bump threatens to give that wedding dress some unexpected curves.

Alison, 25, has been with her boyfriend Dan for almost three years now. Their son is 14 months old and gorgeous, and they're not married. And while she admits she'd like to do it, she's completely certain that not tying the knot has had no impact on their parenting skills at all. 'I'm not married – my boyfriend hasn't asked me,' she says:

> We're not really at that stage yet. I was fine with having our baby before we were married, so were my parents. His really want us to get married, they're quite old-fashioned. It's mostly because they know I'd say yes – I think they think he's being dishonourable towards me by not doing it. I think getting married would be fun, and I really want to have a big party. It will be romantic, I think, and I hope we do it eventually. I like the idea of committing to each other and getting all our friends out to witness it. We're already committed, of course – our son is a blood commitment, which is very strong, and we'll always be in each other's lives. We love our son and I know for sure we'll both do the absolute best for him that we can. But marriage is about wanting to, not about duty. If we get married it'll be about us as people, not us as parents.

Sim, 34, and Tom, 35, are parents to six-month-old Oliver. Not only are they not married, they have no intention of getting married, and they're pretty sure that their decision will have no negative impact on their son at all: 'We're raising our child together and that wouldn't be any different if we were married.' Sim explains:

> Oliver is too young for it to impact negatively on him, although we do get some nasty comments for not being married, especially since he came along. People seem to have a problem with him not having the same surname as me. But

that would be a silly reason for us to go and get married. How can you influence society's attitude to marriage if you're not prepared to question it?

Kids: not just for happy heteros any more!

These new meta-marital modes of parenting aren't restricted to women who got pregnant by feckless exes, men whose wives turned out to be nutters, love-soaked thirtysomethings who want to adopt the world or libertarian couples who choose not to get married. The question of gay people adopting kids is a big one, sure to raise hackles on both sides of the fence whenever it's brought up. (No prizes for guessing which end of the debate I stand on.) As there's still a nasty link in the public imagination between homosexuality, perversion and paedophilia, it can be a downright miracle when gay people get to realise their dreams of parenthood.

Brazil may not be the most politically far left of nations, but a judge's decision in 2006 to allow two gay men to adopt a young girl heralded a quiet revolution. Gay women have been able to adopt children for a while so this case is notable for a double whammy – not only does it signify an increased tolerance for and mainstreaming of same-sex lifestyles, it also illustrates how fathers as primary parents are becoming normalised.

Vasco Pedro de Gama had already adopted five-year-old Theodora on his own. After the case in the state of Sao Paulo the name of his partner of 14 years, Junior de Carvalho, was added to her birth certificate. Theodora had been living with her parents since the previous December, when de Gama began the process to adopt her as a single father. And while the case is a step forward for equality in sexual orientation, more importantly it also allowed one child to be placed in a loving secure home. As their lawyer said at the time, 'If they had tried to adopt as a couple, probably Theodora would not be with them now.'

Surely being raised by a two-father family who have had the commitment and maturity to stay together for 14 long years without being legally bound by a marriage contract bodes infinitely better for her future than being returned to whatever depressing agency she came from, no matter how unusual or perverse some people may find her parents' lifestyle? If we're to truly put the rights of children ahead as more than lip service to an obsessive ideal of unnecessary sacrifice, if we're to truly advocate a *healthy* kind of unselfishness, then it makes complete sense for us to be willing to lay aside our prejudices and preconceptions in favour of securing a child's stable home.

But in a turn of events that is completely unsurprising, not all segments of society have managed to be so admirably forward-thinking about the issue. It took the question of gay adoption to get various strands of Christianity in the United Kingdom to stand together. In January 2007 the government, in an impressive move that was probably motivated more by concern for the pink vote than by thoughts of equality, attempted to push the issue of equal adoption rights for gay couples.

This was part of the Equality Act of 2006 forbidding the refusal of services to anyone on the basis of age, disability, gender, race or religion. The final third of the Act, the one in question that had at the time of writing yet to be approved, extends the same protection to lesbian, gay and bisexual people. And of course it covers adoption agencies along with schools and businesses. Appalled, the Church of England threw its weight behind the Catholic Church (in a move that would have shocked generations of monarchs) and insisted that the 'personal conscience' of Christians was being threatened and that Christian adoption agencies would by no means consider gay couples as prospective parents for the kids in their care. Because, as we all know, gay people are sick perverts and their relationships are abominations. And allowing kids to be raised by queers might offend the delicate sensibilities of the devout and loving Catholic parents who are, er, giving them up for adoption. Or, as Cardinal Cormac Murphy-O'Connor, head of the Catholic Church in England and Wales, put it, 'Marital love involves an essential complementarity of male and female.'[17] (But what if one of you dresses up?)

The Church of England's Archbishop of York, John Sentamu, told a radio interviewer that the Church was 'absolutely' against discrimination and also did not believe homosexuality was a sin, but insisted, 'The freedom of conscience cannot be made subject to legislation however well-meaning.' The Catholic Cardinal also suggested that, if pressed, the Church would have to close its adoption agencies rather than allow same-sex couples to get their filthy hands on the innocent children. Which is clever – that'll *definitely* be the best thing for the kids in question. Why let them get adopted by someone whose lifestyle you don't approve of when you could abandon them to rot in a care home instead?

The Churches seem to be taking the same knee-jerk stand on the issue of gay adoption that they would have taken on single people adopting 20 years ago, or on heterosexual cohabitation 30 years ago. Which means that it's only a matter of time before this too becomes an everyday occurrence, swept along by the tide of social change and development that a reactionary morality based on past principles can do nothing to stem. Things are as they are; the world is changing.

And so, back to skinning cats. How you bring up your children is your choice (unless you're planning to sell them to the highest bidder as soon as they hit 15, in which case you might want to consider getting a hamster and some therapy instead). There is no doubt that having two loving parents is the healthiest, and luckiest, situation for a kid to grow up in, but sometimes it just doesn't work out like that. Children are abused and emotionally damaged by their married parents all the time; less conventional families create responsible, moral, loving and worthwhile human beings all the time.

Things can go nightmarishly wrong within a traditional family grouping. Being married to someone of the opposite sex is no guarantee that you'll make a decent mum or dad, or that you'll make good co-parents, in the same way that choosing or being forced to have your kids outside of marriage does not mean that you're irresponsible, selfish, stupid, amoral and unfit. It's all too easy when considering kids to fall victim to the guilt mentality that insists that unless we do it the 'right' way we're causing them some irreparable wrong. And the big question, of course, is who wrote that particular book, who decided which was the right way and which the wrong way?

Not so very long ago it would have been considered bizarre to live in an insular nuclear family, with just mum and dad and Sally and John and Spot the golden retriever. Until fairly recently in human history families were extended, communities essential, and children had moral and emotional input from more than just their parents. Grandparents, aunts, uncles and all flavour of relatives were involved. But the nuclear model has come to seem so orthodox that many prospective or current parents live in shame and fear that they've damaged their children by daring to do it differently. That's true even though the statistics bear out that poverty and lack of education – which are admittedly all too often the conditions for undesired single parenthood – are more to blame for these children's later problems than the marital status of their parents. If you're poor and have barely been to school and get knocked up by the local crack dealer then no, you're not a good poster child for parenthood outside of marriage, but having a kid really wasn't the start of your problems. If you're one of the luckier ones, educated and self-aware and not beset by poverty, then your child will have a decent shot at life, married parents or not.

Philip Larkin hit the nail on the head in his poem 'This be the verse' when he admitted that your mother and father, inevitably, fuck you up. No matter what you do, you'll do something wrong. Too many of us are panicking about being perfect parents, trying to run around in pinafores and faultless curls and making flawless casseroles, or coaching Little League and taking Jimmy out to the garage to saw a plank of wood in half.

Marriage is a serious commitment and a serious choice. Diving into it as an automatic response to the desire to have a family is irresponsible and careless – and our children, I think you'll agree, deserve better than that.

Chapter Six

'I don't want to be alone'

Of the many reasons for marriage given by this book's many interviewees this was by far the most heartbreaking, and the hardest to argue with. How do you convince someone that there are worse things than solitude, that being legally bound to a person who's all wrong for you can be a sentence without parole, whereas being on your own is a state that can be changed at any time, should the chance arise?[1]

Never mind the fact that being alone really isn't that bad. Time by yourself, as anyone who's ever gone on a retreat, run away to the countryside or even lived solo will tell you, can be healing, calming, energising, pleasing, a momentary escape from the mania of the world and a valuable space to reflect and grow that's unlike any other.

We also need to bear in mind the unpleasant possibility that people who live in fear of being alone often do so because they can't handle their own company. You can fit in as many yoga classes as your hectic schedule will allow, but if you're not capable of spending a few days or even a few hours with yourself then you're seriously lacking in zen, and all the stretchy hamstrings in the world won't help your sense of inner peace. Being comfortable with yourself is a lot more difficult than it may sound to those who do it naturally. But hey, we live and learn – if we stick too close to our comfort zones we'll never develop. And this is part of the life lesson that lurks within the pervasive and unpleasant fear of being alone. It's not something to be pandered to, it's something to be gone through and emerged from, stronger, braver and wiser.

But before we get too far into the inspirational Oprah talk, which I admit does raise my cynical hackles somewhat, let's start with a horror story or two, just to keep the balance. I'll give you the less terrifying one first to let you get used to it.

Louise is in her late 30s and divorced. An artist, she's been living in Berlin for the past five years where she's part of a vibrant creative community. While she doesn't have much money, she's happy – especially in comparison with her life before she moved.

She says, 'I went to art school in Birmingham,[2] which is near to where I grew up and where my parents still live. I'm a painter, which even back when I was a student wasn't the most exciting or modern discipline. But it suited me because I was terribly shy and I would have felt really uncomfortable if I'd done any of the more showy things, like sculpture or installation. After uni I got a job in an office but I kept painting, just doing it quietly at home, more for my own pleasure than because I thought it would go anywhere. I was quite content with my quiet little life, I had my friends from school and uni and my family nearby, and I never really felt the urge to break away like most people did.

'That all changed the year before I turned 30. Both my sisters, who are older, had got married, and one already had kids. I'd had boyfriends, nice lads who treated me well, but there were never any fireworks. That year my sisters started teasing me about being an old maid, which of course is totally ridiculous; this was in the 90s and things weren't like that any more, but I got worried and panic-stricken that I was never going to meet anybody and all I would have would be this life of going to work and coming home and making paintings no one would ever see.

'So I suppose I kind of decided that I wanted to get married, settle down and start the "adult" part of my life. It was a crazy idea. I was still a child in so many ways because I had been living this insular life, and I hadn't matured even though I was not that young. I set about this project in the most ridiculous ways. I started wearing make-up and got a hairstyle for the first time, and started wearing skirts to work. Which obviously is not the way to meet your soulmate but I had got it into my head that it was my own fault I was alone and all I needed to do was make some effort.

'I met my husband-to-be quite soon. My firm did some business with him. He asked me if I wanted to go for a pint, and that was our first date. He was a lot older than me, I was 29 and he was about 40, and he had never been married. I probably should have wondered about that but I didn't. I also should have wondered why he was interested in me: I was hardly a stunner and I didn't even talk much. I was bit dazzled because he had money, not huge amounts but more than I was used to. He took me to nice restaurants and seemed to enjoy being with me. I never did much except sit there and smile, which should really have been a clue to how our marriage would end up.'

After what they traditionally call a whirlwind courtship Louise was duly swept off her feet and proposed to, just a few months after that earth-shattering 30th birthday.

'My husband expected me to stop working as soon as we were married,' she continues. 'I was a bit surprised at that and I missed everyone at the office, but I saw it as a chance to do more painting, which was wonderful for me. Except he didn't see it that way at all, he wanted me to be a full-time housewife.

I moved into the house he already owned. It wasn't to my taste at all, it was very much a bachelor's house and I wanted to change it, but he wouldn't let me. He just wanted me to keep it clean and tidy and to have meals ready on the table for him when he got home. I don't know how he thought I would fill up my days other than that, but he probably never considered it much.'

Though she tried to enter into the spirit of the marriage, Louise soon found herself frustrated at not being able to paint. She made contact with a friend from art school who had lots of studio space, and she spent many of her days there.

'Until he made me stop I never realised just how important my art is to me,' she says. 'Even though I'd done a degree I always thought of it as a hobby. But after my marriage I felt so constricted and bound up, I could hardly breathe, and that wasn't just because my husband was bossy and controlling. By taking it away he really made me see how important it was. So there was no big blow-up or anything, just a slow process of me realising I couldn't possibly be with someone who denied me that.'

She stuck it out for almost two years, but eventually, and with little fanfare, Louise left her husband without bearing him the children he wanted. Her friends and family were mostly 'confused' by her uncharacteristic behaviour, but supportive. A few years later she moved to Berlin after an inspiring visit to an artists' collective there.

She says, 'I don't bear my ex-husband any ill will. In a lot of ways the disaster of my marriage helped me to find myself. Moving [to Germany] was a really good decision and I wouldn't have done it before, although that could also have had something to do with me getting older. I was such a little mouse in my 20s, it makes me sad to think of now.

'I actually feel quite sorry for him. He married a girl who was very quiet and shy and submissive, and he thought she'd stay like that for the rest of his and her lives. Why anyone would want to be married to someone who's scared to open their mouth I don't know, but that's what he wanted. During our marriage I went from being that person to being me, and a big part of the reason is that he stopped me doing what I loved, and that made me angry. So yes, I'm kind of grateful to him. He did me a big favour. Grateful and glad that I'm not married to him!

'I get sad sometimes because I wonder whether I'll get to have kids and whether I'll find someone I really want to be with. I think I screwed up by wasting my 20s like that. But you have to be grateful for what you have, and my life now is a lot more interesting than my life before.'

OK, so not that much of a horror story, and it worked out well for Louise if not for her ex. But she is one of the lucky ones.

I found Trish, now in her 40s, via an ad I placed on an online women's forum. Unlike most of my respondents she didn't want to enter into any kind of discussion. She didn't want me to ask her questions or explain my project, she just wanted to tell her story and have done.

'I wanted to get married and have a big family, and it felt like I was running out of time to meet someone on my own so I decided to be proactive. A friend suggested internet dating as a good way to find a husband so I signed up to a Christian website as this looked like it would be the safest place. I had a lot of responses and replied to a few men, some of whom were very nice and some not great. The nicest one was called John. He happened to spend a lot of time on the road in an area near my home town so we arranged to meet.

'The date went very well and we saw each other a lot more over the next few months. We also communicated by email during this time. I was not in love with him by any means but he seemed like a decent and kind person with good values, and as I say I wanted to start a family, so I decided he was the best option. I did not have any romantic illusions that we would fall in love but I thought we could make a good home together and be partners in our lives.

'When we got married I moved away to where he lived which meant I did not have people I knew around me. Very quickly I realised I did not really know this man I was living with. He was sexually aggressive, which is not what you expect from a Christian, and he also drank. When he was drunk he used to hit me. I never had broken ribs or bones but I often had a shiner and would wear dark sunglasses. Since I did not know anyone around there was no one to be concerned for me and I felt so foolish and ashamed that I never asked for help from home. I did actually get pregnant which made me extremely happy, but I lost the baby. I think it was from stress and worry.

'Eventually I started going to church and I got to know the priest there. He was very good to me and helped me get the strength to see that what had happened was not my fault. The people at the church all helped me make the difficult decision to leave my husband. Once I had done it I could not believe I had stayed there for so long. We are now in the process of getting a divorce which he is contesting, and it's difficult to prove the abuse because I never called the police or went to hospital. But the people at my church are helping me and so is my family, and soon I hope to have put this nightmare behind me.'

Bit more horrific, yes? But what they have in common is a sense that both Louise and Trish had so little idea of their own value that they were willing to auction themselves off to the first bidder. It's about as far as possible as you can get from romantic marriage, where both people believe that a mystical, magical star-struck partnership 'as seen on TV' is their God-given right and nothing else will do. These women set no store by their own company, their own place in the world, and were battered by the desire to attach themselves to someone of greater substance – that someone being, of course, a man, who would function effectively in the wider world in a way that they never could.

Both women were unfortunate in their choice of husbands, where I suppose it's possible that they could as easily have been luckier; but a passive, submissive attitude to one's own life tends to attract people who want to dominate. And people who want to dominate in the home often do so, in my meagre experience, because they can't outside. Men who beat their wives are often frustrated by their lack of agency in the outside world and eager for someone, anyone, weaker to display their power on. So in general women like Trish and Louise, with their near-minimal standards and low expectations, are more likely to attract tormentors than the protectors they hope for. If they're lucky they'll find new strength in the experience; if they're not, it may break them. In either case it would have been far better not to get married and to expend their emotional energies on themselves rather than on Mr Extremely Wrong.

Of course, as is the case with anyone else's tale, these stories are particular to their owners. Go ahead, dismiss them if you will. It's easy to do, easy to assume that you know better than to get into situations like these. But people do; sensible, stable people make these kinds of choices *all the time*. For *all the wrong reasons*. It seems that sometimes marrying someone because you're scared of being alone is the only thing that can teach you the value of being alone. Not that I'm suggesting the more insecure among you go out and try it.

Women and the imaginary age barrier

Before we continue, a warning – there's some unpleasant stuff ahead and you may want to look away now. Expect contention, opinion, ranting, snap judgements and loosely backed-up statements of fact. As the more astute among you may have noticed during the course of reading this book, deeply unfashionable though it be, your author has a few – don't faint now – feminist leanings. No, not the sort of feminism that involves castrating all men (although if there was a way to do it temporarily between the ages of 14 and 17 I'd probably approve), or the sort of feminism that involves burning your bra. As anyone who's met me can testify, I would be lost without my bra. No, rather it's the sort of feminism that's pro-woman, pro women having the same expanse of choice and freedom as men, without turning men into emasculated apron-wearing bunny boys. I know, crazy idea, one that would probably shock the braying anti-feminist brigade, but there you go – I like to live on the edge.[3]

The fact is, sadly, that the fear of getting old alone is a peculiarly female paranoia. Heard the one about the old man who died in his apartment and got eaten by his Alsatians because no one noticed? No? Thought not. How about the one about the old man who shares his flat with 20 cats? Or the one about the weird old man who wanders around talking to himself and the local kids think he's a witch? No? Hmm. Funny. I wonder whether this gross oversight could have anything to do with the fact that age carries a stigma for women that it doesn't hold for men, and that solitary old age is the great terror of the unmarried 35-year-old woman. (It's getting better; used be 25-year-olds grappling with that particular hook.) Men don't live in terror that time is running out; with women it's a constant theme.

This is one of the great challenges that faces educated first-world women today – fine, you have the career, but when are you going to have time to get the husband and the kids if it takes you till age 35 to really cement your working life? There is undeniably a biological component to this. If you want to have children you have to do it before a certain age (although that age is getting later and later, which bodes nothing but well for female freedom).

As I said in the discussion on the physiognomy of love in Chapter One, it's bizarre and slightly unsettling that we as a species make so much effort to free ourselves from the chains of our biology until it comes to love, sex and reproduction. Take vegetarianism – very common today, with some religions even requiring it. But our basic animal nature dictates that we're omnivores, so in a sense not eating meat is a crime against our primal urges; it's *unnatural behaviour*. You don't, however, find censorious journalists mouthing off about 'irresponsible' vegetarians the way they do about women who choose not to have children in their 20s – the peak child-bearing years, or so we're told.

In 2006, in fact, the United States unleashed new federal guidelines in which all women of childbearing age are to be considered something called 'pre-pregnant' and expected to behave accordingly.[4] *All* women. Whether you plan to have kids or not, the fact that you're in possession of a womb means your body is not your own; it is a potential incubator for a potential voter. According to the government's report on the subject, 'during the first few weeks of pregnancy' – when you may not know you've been knocked up – 'exposure to alcohol, tobacco and other drugs; lack of essential vitamins (eg folic acid); and workplace hazards can adversely affect foetal development and result in pregnancy complications and poor outcomes for both the mother and the infant'.

See what that says? That says that you shouldn't drink alcohol. Just in case. Ever. Until the menopause. Because you might get pregnant by accident. Well, I tell you, you can have my bottle of Jameson Irish Whiskey when you prise it from my cold dead hand. My body is not a temple to anyone's wishes but my own, and nor should it be.

Objectifying women's physiology like this means that we are become legally understood as being potential mothers because our bodies have the ability to bear children, but it also completely discounts our minds, our individual wills, any consideration that just because a human being is born with the knack of carrying a baby she might not choose to, or want to, or be quite ready to. This, my friends, is the kind of state-run insanity that happens when we let biology control the decisions we make about our lives.[5] So yes, if you want to have kids and a career you're in something of a pickle. But it can be done with a little luck and effort, and it will get easier the more women have decent jobs and force their employers to make concessions for childcare and flexible working.

But will those changes, which are in the wind already, have any effect on the persistent idea that growing old alone is a particularly female affliction, one that women must fear and avoid at all costs, even to the point of marrying a relative stranger just because he's there? What we're talking about here is not low self-esteem or the kind of loathing that comes with being terrified of spending time with oneself. No, what we're talking about here is the social censure that women face when they hit a certain age and they haven't been paired off yet.

Don't believe me? OK, try this little trick. 'Bachelor. Spinster. Bachelor. Spinster.' Go on, say them aloud and gauge your responses. One sounds kind of glamorous, right? And the other about as dowdy and pinched as it's possible to get. Now admittedly the second word – I can't write it again, it makes me come over all funny – is not in common use much any more, but it's not been replaced with anything as footloose and fancy-free as 'bachelor'. Language tells a story; the fact that we have a word for a functional fun and funky single male but not the equivalent for a single female indicates that there's still some resistance to this concept. Because women, as they get older, get less attractive, less appealing, less fuckable. Men don't. And this isn't unfortunate biological fact either; it's all down to training, to what we've learned from movies, magazines, books, our societies.

Take, for example, a selection of lonely hearts adverts, picked from UK newspaper the *Guardian*'s Soulmates section on 10 March 2007 (in case you suspect I'm making them up). A 62-year-old male teacher who enjoys the outdoors as well as intellectual hobbies looked for a woman aged 45 to 55. An urbane-sounding former musician, writer, singer and poet in his early 60s looked for an attractive woman in her late 40s. A quirky and amusing 50-year-old looked for a 'princess' aged between 30 and 45 to turn him into a prince. I could go on but you can probably see what I'm getting at (and I won't even start talking about the 'slim' requirement that crept into all three ads, that's a whole different kettle of fish). What these men have in common is a desire for a woman significantly younger than themselves.

They're in luck; let's matchmake our eligible bachelors with some fine fillies from the women's column of the same paper. An independent and intelligent 58-year-old woman with varied interests looked for a man aged between 58 and 65 to enjoy life with. A glamorous and well-travelled lady in her 60s was after a cultured man of 60 to 75. A Russian beauty in her early 40s wanted a good-looking gent of 42 to 52. There, I think that went quite well (except for the last pair, they're never going to work out). The common thread? Older. They all want older men.

I'm not suggesting that every personal ad ever posted has these specific requirements, and I admit that my methods are rather unscientific. Of course you can't completely extrapolate the prejudices in modern society from three pages in a newspaper; but for the sake of argument allow me to make the point anyway. Many of the ads in that day's paper mentioned their own age but not their hoped-for lover's; indeed, there were a few on the women's side that requested men aged from ten years below up to their own ages, although the usual trend with women seemed to be to set the age limit about two years younger and eight older. There was not, however, a single woman seeking a man a *minimum* of a decade younger than her. On the men's side the ads that did mention age tended to err in a similar fashion while going slightly further in the opposite direction, with the predisposition being to limit one's partner's age from ten years younger up to one's own.

The only time age limits above the male advertiser's own were given was in 'speciality' ads, when 'naughty' or 'wicked' young men in their 20s and early 30s advertised for 'passionate' and 'sensual' older women. So if your taste in men runs to the younger, much as the men's ads quoted here do in terms of women, your only option is a blatantly sexual relationship with someone who actually refers to himself as 'young', forgoing all the romance and conversation promised by the other men advertising on the same page in favour of engaging with someone purely on a sexual level.

And as a man, if you find women your own age unstimulating, your desire to date someone older will automatically place you in the 'naughty but nice' Mrs Robinson-loving category. Which is not exactly fair to anyone.

That said, for everyone other than these unfortunate deviants it seems to work out perfectly – the men in their 60s get the women in their 50s, all the way down to men in their 20s dating 18-year-old girls, and everyone's happy. Except for one little thing. What about the women in their 60s? Must they date men in their 70s? What if mid-70s is too old for a sprightly 60-something who's only recently retired and is ready to start enjoying her life? What if she wants someone her own age, who's at her own stage in life? Ah well, she's a bit buggered then – she shouldn't have got divorced.

The cult of youth, while it doubtless affects men to some extent, draws its lifeblood from tramping on the faces of women who hit the dreaded 40s without retaining a Sharon Stone-like physical perfection. UK journalist Kathryn Flett calls it the 'Invisible Middle years', that period of your life when people suddenly start looking through you in public because you have no sexual presence.[6] None. Nada. This is the time, Flett writes, when you:

> privately fantasise about infanticide in the frozen food aisle when, say, a cute man we suddenly, shockingly, realise is ten years our junior fails, equally shockingly, to acknowledge our existence while we're both reaching for the baby broad beans. Invisibility creeps up on you unawares. If you hit your 40s child-free, botoxed and with an ashtanga-ed arse, then you'll delay it a while, but it's still just a matter of time.

Now that sounds like something to look forward to. And the thing is, *this just doesn't happen* to men. Men get more distinguished, more interesting even, no matter how many hairs start sprouting from their ears. Men do not disappear into a grey asexual limbo in their 40s; their 40s are wonderful. That may be slowly shifting as the metrosexual revolution has all the blokes we know reaching for the Clinique, but it's unlikely to change completely, and the reason is that most positions of power are still held by men who are not judged on their physical attractiveness.

In general women are valued on the basis of what they look like because there's still an underlying social assumption, whether we're aware of it or not, that their appearance is their major currency, the one bartering tool they have to offer in a vicious market. Bill Gates is no oil painting, but no one looks through him. An older man is not dismissed on the basis of how sexually attractive he is because he may have all sorts of other things to recommend him, and indeed to *make* him sexually attractive, like huge amounts of money and legions of scurrying underlings. It's unfortunate, and a good slap in the face for those women who still insist that feminism has done its job and should go away, but that's the way it is – for now, at least.

Until we get used to seeing middle-aged women in the public eye who aren't actresses and thus far better looking than most of us (and actresses have their problems too once they cross the invisible dividing line between fresh and past it), this will not change. Sir Alan Sugar and Donald Trump – not wildly attractive men, but that's hardly the first thought in anyone's head as they strut their stuff on TV in *The Apprentice*. Where are the women of comparable age with comparable looks? They're hiding because, as everyone knows, an unattractive woman has no right to torture the world by making it look at her.

The older a woman gets the closer she comes to invisibility; it's harsh and it's depressing but it's still true. And it's no wonder, then, that so many women fear getting old alone, when ageing condemns you to vanishing in society's eyes. You'd better have a partner before it gets too late or not only will you never get laid again, ever, you'll spend the rest of your life cleaning kitty litter boxes! Mwahahahahaha! Dickens' mad and malicious Miss Havisham, from *Great Expectations*, is many women's bogeyman under the stairs, living in the wreck of her aborted wedding and doing her cackling, insane best to punish every man she can get her claws on for the pain of being abandoned back when she was still fresh, young and marriageable.

The fame age game

In case you don't believe me about these stigmatic gender assumptions, let's take another brief look at the all-knowing, all-telling celebrity barometer of our times. First up there's the age question, which as we've seen impacts quite heavily on the pressure on women to pair up before they're past it. The following are two lists of the sexiest stars around in 2006 and their ages at the time of writing, the first from American *FHM* and the second from *People* magazine.

Scarlett Johansson (22)
Angelina Jolie (31)
Jessica Alba (25)
Jessica Simpson (26)
Keira Knightley (21)
Halle Berry (40)
Jenny McCarthy (34)
Maria Sharapova (19)
Carmen Electra (34)
Teri Hatcher (42)
Paris Hilton (26)
Jennifer Garner (34)
Eva Longoria (32)
Lindsay Lohan (20)
Charlize Theron (31)

George Clooney (45)
Patrick Dempsey (41)
Ashton Kutcher (29)
Taye Diggs (36)
Johnny Depp (43)
Josh Duhamel (34)
Enrique Murciano (33)
Leonardo DiCaprio (32)
Josh Krasinski (27)
Jake Gyllenhaal (26)
John Cho (34)
Rodrigo Santoro (31)
Omar Epps (33)
Eric Mabius (35)
Brad Pitt (43)

The women have a combined age of 437 and an average of 29 – but this is pushed up by the presence of Teri Hatcher and Halle Berry, both of whom are significantly older than the majority of the lucky ladies. There are seven in their teens and 20s, six in their early 30s and just two in their 40s, early at that. The men are at 522 years combined with an average age of 35, not a massive increase; but if you take a look at the differential between them it's much more evenly spaced, with three in their late 20s, eight spread across their 30s and four in various stages of their 40s.

These lists tell us a number of things. Not only that men are seen to be sexier when they're older, and that teenage or just post-teenage boys are not considered legitimate lust objects they way that girls are, but that men remain sexy all through these three decades,[7] whereas it's fairly unusual for women in their 40s to make this kind of list. When they do they're the exceptions rather than the rules, and female sexiness is heavily weighted towards the 20s. As many women in their 30s and 40s attest, it's only when you leave this stage of life that you begin to hit your peak, more confident and more sure of yourself and wiser and more interesting, even though your breasts may be getting something of a sag to them. It's a great irony that this is approximately when the world's interest in your sexual value begins to wane.

I think we can safely conclude that physical attraction, for women, is to a large extent dependent on youth. If you know you're going to be past it as soon as the crow's feet start to show in sunlight, then naturally you're going feel a fairly intense pressure to bag someone, anyone, while you still have something going for yourself. Leaving aside questions of child-bearing and fertility, when most of the paragons of female beauty that we are shown on a daily basis are under 35 (sometimes way under), it's hardly surprising that women over 35 are pawning their kidneys to pay for face peels and La Prairie skin-care. And it's even less surprising that those women who haven't already snagged a mate are descending into *Bridget Jones*-like paranoia while they quaff their chardonnay and sob on their married friends' shoulders. But don't take my word for it – let's go back to Celebville and look at how the great and the good deal with the problem of settling down once the dew of the early 20s has faded from their botoxed brows.

Can anyone claim that George Clooney, hunk of the decade and long-confirmed bachelor that he is, has the same vague whiff of desperation hanging around him as the perennially single Teri Hatcher, also in her 40s? A large part of the reason for this is reportage, the kind of terminology used when describing the two actors, both by the press and, sadly, by themselves.

Hatcher is a 'single mom' who's known for being 'unlucky in love'. She's made her way through a few Hollywood hotties in her time, not least Clooney himself by some accounts, but the way she's spoken of and the way she speaks of herself point to the fact that she's had a hard time with romance, that she's suffered at the hands of men. Admitting to childhood sexual abuse, Hatcher said, 'I am a woman who carries around all these layers of fear and vulnerability. The biggest effect to me is this area of love and men, which hasn't been so great.'[8] When her fledgling romance with Ryan Seacrest ended after a fateful paparazzi shot of them kissing scared him off, she said, 'Everyone clearly knows about my pathetic single dating life, right?'

Now this is a beautiful, wealthy, successful woman who's cut something of a swathe through the heartthrobs of her day. And we should be feeling *sorry* for her? Somehow that doesn't sit right. All of the media trumpeting about her renewed success in her fifth decade is tempered with a slight patronising tone of sympathy for the woman who's so neurotic that she can't keep a man. She's painted in a victimised hue that may well be appropriate to her personality but, I'm convinced, has just as much to do with still being single at her advanced age. She's obviously looking for a man, seeking Mr Right, that good old prince on his good old horse, and none of her other achievements quite override this element of her persona in the popular conception.

Clooney, on the other hand, is the diametric opposite. OK, so he doesn't talk publicly about wanting to settle down, but again I contend that this has much to do with the fact that he doesn't have to. He's freed from the expectations of marriage and commitment because he's a man. His failure to commit to one woman is translated into the popular culture as being roguish, dashing, charming rather than tragic. Divorced from actress Talia Balsam before his star shone as brightly as it does now, Clooney has dated a tabloid 'string of beauties' but was generally painted as being more devoted to his pot-bellied pig Max until that animal's untimely death. Nicole Kidman and Michelle Pfeiffer bet him a pile of money that he'd be married by age 50 and he seems to be doing his best to get the cash – and this well-known gambling story only adds to his allure. Rather than an aura of desperation he maintains a sense of being untameable: attractive and independent and solitary. Never for a moment does his lifestyle invoke the slightest shred of pity – he's an object of envy more than anything else.

Being single in your 40s when you're male reads like a choice, like James Bond, like a decision you've made which you can revoke whenever you feel like it, seeing as how men don't lose their appeal the further they get from puberty. Being single in your 40s when you're female, however, inevitably comes with a sense that it's your fate because you could not find a man. There's no question of choice for women or of bad luck for men. And it's not fair. But it's changing.

Take action

And so we come to the crux of this chapter. As we've seen, the fear of ageing alone is a peculiarly feminine ailment, like hysteria and bad-hair days (although these are fast being adopted by the boys too). Add to that the pressure on women to find someone 'before it's too late' and the general trend of older men dating younger women – leaving the older women in some kind of impenetrable limbo – and it's not surprising that so many modern ladies are finding the dating and mating game just the slightest bit tense.

As well as all the usual pressure to get married that we encountered in Chapter Five, women have the added bonus of facing eventual haggery if they don't find someone who's willing to trot to the nearest altar with them before their highlights fade and the grey starts to show. It's not a pretty picture. The question is, what do we do about it? Set up all-inclusive dating agencies? Make more of an effort to help our poor single friends get paired off asap? Invest in pro-homosexual psychology techniques, so we can turn all the women left on the shelf into lesbians and couple them up with each other?

Diverting as these pastimes may prove to be, the answer's a lot simpler. What we do is change attitudes, our own and everyone else's. We work to eradicate the perception that a single woman is somehow half a person. We try as hard as possible not to fall into the trap of sneering at older women and thinking of them as mutton dressed as lamb if they dare to do anything other than huddle quietly in the corner with their knitting. We think twice before accepting everything we read in magazines, and acknowledge that those photos are airbrushed anyway and no one looks that good in reality. We effect a dramatic paradigm shift in ourselves and in those we know. We change methods of understanding. We relearn to see things with our eyes rather than with the jaundiced view of the press. We start thinking again, for ourselves this time, and we start to see people as people rather than as demographics. And when this happens we relax, because suddenly we're part of the solution, not the problem.

That said, no one can really do a damn thing about anyone else's low self-esteem, but if that's your issue you can take it in hand, consider how and why you ended up with these feelings, how they affect you, what they mean. If you find yourself so desperate to be with someone that you end up with an obviously wrong person then you need to work out what it was you were expecting from them, how you thought they'd validate or justify or improve your life, and how they've failed you or you've failed yourself. Once you've looked at yourself very carefully and understood why you make the choices you make perhaps you can start to lean towards healthier decisions, decisions that really do have the desired effect, that make you happier and give you more security.

But the most important thing to keep in mind is that no one else can kickstart that process. It's internal, it has to come from you or it'll never work. You can't depend on anyone else to fill the holes you may have in your heart, and until you work through them yourself, your relationships will always be lacking. Marrying someone because you think they'll make you less lonely is no answer. Until you're happy with yourself you won't be happy with them. As obvious as it sounds, it's a trick a lot of people are missing.

Chapter Seven

'Marriage means you're committed'

Being committed means never having to say you're sorry. Yup, that's right kids – just run off and get that official seal of church and state approval™ and nothing will ever go wrong in your relationship again. No really, it's true, I promise. Get married and you'll be committed for life, no questions asked, till death do you part, just like in the movies. What's that you say? Oh, don't worry, just ignore that pesky divorce lawyer. What does he know? He's nothing but a bitter, angry and insanely rich little man who's jealous of the purity of your love. Why yes *of course* you can have a pony. Let's just wait till the Easter Bunny arrives and ask him to deliver one, OK?

Indeed, the road to hell is paved with good intentions. I suspect that most people who wind up as nasty statistics get married with the intention of staying together; that doesn't, however, mean they can pull it off. It's no mean feat. And if you're committed to your partner you'll remain committed whether you have a 200-person wedding in the Sheraton Hotel, a Wiccan handfasting ceremony in a wood or just a day-to-day life you're both satisfied with. Sad but true, getting married doesn't make you any more committed. Sure, it can make the relationship more difficult to get out of, but since when did that equate to commitment? 'Well, we're locked into this thing and it's too much effort to get out, so I guess I love you.' Nice.

This is one of the most nonsensical reasons people give for getting married, as if a ceremony or a party or the sight of your friends and family bearing witness will somehow cement and fortify an emotional contract that you and your partner have made. Perhaps these people believe that anything they don't say publicly isn't true, and so as long as you haven't officially informed the world at large that you intend to stay with your partner, you have a permanent 'get out of jail free' card lurking up your sleeve.

Plenty of people manage to stay together for long periods of time without the need for official certification. If you're getting married as a romantic gesture to illustrate how committed you are, well that's lovely, and I'll direct you to Chapter Three where you can think about just how desperately you really need that wedding. If, however, your desires are more insidious and you want to get married because that will *make* you committed, you're both naïve and foolish. The decision to stay with someone is one you make every day. If the difficulties of divorce are all that keep you together, you'd be better off not marrying at all and moving on to a stage in your life that doesn't involve tying your emotional well-being to a legal contract. A marriage does not, and never will, mean that you're committed. Attempting to make it so is like standing at the top of a tall building and flapping your arms very hard in the hopes that that'll make you fly. It's not the way of the world, you see – you flap because you can soar like a birdie, you don't learn to soar like a birdie because you've done so much flapping.

Commitment and a life shared are things you will attain through hard work and dedication and not a small amount of luck. You will not get them because you hired the best caterer around and managed not to sleep with anyone else on your stag or hen weekend. Like a plaster applied to a gaping wound, marriage will not hold together something that couldn't survive alone. There's a fair chance that all you're really doing is setting yourself up for an unpleasant few years and one of those hideous divorces so beloved of the supermarket tabloids.

A brief history of divorce

While we're on the subject, let's have a little think about divorce. It's nothing new in Western Europe – the ancient Athenians permitted themselves to back out of marriage when necessary, if sanctioned by a magistrate. When the Roman Empire was at its peak civil law adopted the motto '*matrimonia debent esse libera*': marriages ought to be free, which meant that either spouse could dissolve their union. Casual divorce was uncommon, mostly because social and religious taboo prohibited it, but nonetheless people did have a legal and acceptable get-out clause.

The Christian emperors Constantine and Theodosius restricted the grounds for divorce, but in the sixth century the more agreeable Justinian relaxed them again. After the fall of the empire the Christian Church was left in charge, meaning divorce was far less common and marriage viewed as a religious testament, something ordained by God that no mere humans had the right to dissolve, even the mere humans who were actually involved in the marriage. Divorce then danced on the far edges of legality for a few centuries, and people were in the main limited to annulment, which was granted only by the power of the Church courts. A marriage in the eyes of God meant that two people 'became one' indivisibly. Annulment was the only option as it meant that one of those people had entered into the marriage under false pretences so the whole thing was a lie from the start. Not much room for the margin of error or a drunken mistake in Vegas. So deeply was the two-into-one belief held that wives, for all practical purposes, actually ceased to exist upon getting married.

According to Sir William Blackstone's *Commentaries on the Laws of England* (1765–69), 'By marriage the husband and wife are one person in law: that is, the very being of legal existence of the woman is suspended during the marriage or at least incorporated and consolidated into that of the husband under whose wing, protection and cover, she performs everything.' As marriage came to be seen as a legal rather than a religious contract, civil authorities and courts eventually began to regulate its legality. But since the only precedent they had for dissolving marriages was the Church's, those were the rules they stuck to and divorce remained a dirty word, granted only in the most extreme cases. So determined were courts to keep to these strictures that divorces were consistently refused in cases where both parties wanted them. If both husband and wife had behaved badly they were punished by being forced to remain in the marriage. The only way to earn a legal separation was if one person violated their 'sacred vow' to their innocent spouse.

In the 1530s England's King Henry VIII joined the Protestants, threw over papal supremacy, founded the Church of England and declared himself its head, setting off decades of internecine religious turmoil, because the Pope refused to let him put aside his wife and marry that saucy temptress Anne Boleyn.[1]

Until 1858 divorce in England could only be obtained by an expensive Act of Parliament. Church courts could grant separations but these forbade either spouse from marrying again, so either you were stuck with what you'd got or left with nothing. Fortunately for all concerned this rigid structure eventually loosened up until it reached its current state, where people who are not happy in their marriages can get out of them without having to engage in the sort of maniacal destructiveness that would have impressed a 17th-century court.

In the 20th century divorce carried its own unpleasant stigma even as it became less transgressive. In Canada, for example, divorce was very rare until well after the end of the Second World War, before which the country had one of the lowest recorded rates. Before the First World War, in fact, only three Canadian states possessed anything as exotic and modern as a divorce court, and adultery was the only legal reason for granting a petition. The strong social pressure of respectability insisted that divorce was a threat to the stability of the family and thus to the structure of society as whole. Divorce was very difficult to do until as late as 1968, so people often resorted to abandoning their spouses, running across the border to the United States to get at least some sort of divorce or having a legal separation which prevented either from remarrying.

The idea of the glamorous divorcee who had her own money (conned out of her clueless ex-husband, of course), smoked cigarettes, drove like a bat out of hell and preyed on happily married men was endemic in the United States in the 1920s and 1930s. She was too fast, too flash and too independent to be acceptable. Women who left their marriages were viewed with suspicion and a smattering of lust by the popular imagination.

It wasn't only in the movie-soaked United States that divorce was considered shocking. All across the Western world, leaving your marriage was a recipe for instant approbation. It was tantamount to admitting that you had no morals. Sanja, 30, relates a horrible tale of her grandmother's life in small-town 1950s' West Germany, a history that resulted in her living the rest of her life as a solitary pariah.

> My granny was the only divorcee in her village. People were literally outraged. The fact that her husband had continually cheated on her, wasted all his own money, then lived off her money and wasted all that too, and still owes her lots of money, all of that was totally irrelevant, they were too busy being disgusted with her. She basically decided, I've had enough. She told me, in her old-fashioned way, that if he had got rid of his mistresses and said sorry, she would have forgiven him, but he wouldn't make the choice between her and the rest of them so she made the choice for him. She asked my mum after the divorce if she wanted to have another daddy, and my mum said no, my daddy or no daddy. But he didn't want to be part of her life, so my gran never had another relationship after that, even though loads of people were interested in her. Her ex-husband never had any contact with my mum, he just started a new family with someone else. I think I saw my granddad once when I was really really tiny and that was the last time he saw my mum. But meantime it was my granny who got all the blame.

Divorce: it's the new black

So yes, in a lot of ways we're lucky, lucky that we can do it without ruining our lives. That said, divorce may have become easier and more common but it's not, in general, pretty. I explained in Chapter Five why it can be a viable option when opposed to staying in a painful and difficult marriage, but that's not to say that it's ever the best possible outcome or one you shouldn't avoid like the plague. And how do we do that? Well, it's the old chicken and egg story. If you didn't get married you'd never have to deal with a messy divorce. And if getting married really meant that you were committed, we wouldn't have the soaring rates we see these days. Divorcemag.com gives the following terrifying list of the percentage of marriages that ended in divorce in 1996, by country:

Belarus	68	Denmark	35
Russian Federation	65	Slovakia	34
Sweden	64	Bulgaria	28
Latvia	63	Israel	26
Ukraine	63	Slovenia	26
Czech Republic	61	Kyrgystan	25
Belgium	56	Romania	24
Finland	56	Portugal	21
Lithuania	55	Poland	19
United Kingdom	53	Armenia	18
Moldova	52	Greece	18
United States	49	Turkmenistan	18
Hungary	46	Spain	17
Canada	45	Azerbaijan	15
Norway	43	Croatia	15
France	43	Cyprus	13
Germany	41	Tajikistan	13
Netherlands	41	Georgia	12
Switzerland	40	Italy	12
Iceland	39	Uzbekistan	12
Kazakhstan	39	Albania	7
Luxemburg	39	Turkey	6
Austria	38	Macedonia	5

That's an awful lot of people who thought they were committed and then somehow figured out that they weren't. We have stars in our eyes and we've failed to learn from our parents' generation's mistake.

According to a recent poll conducted in the UK, 77 per cent of Britons in their first marriage agree that a marital commitment should be for life. Even 66 per cent of cohabiting couples agree, which is probably why they haven't got married. These figures only tail off when you get to divorcees, with 49 per cent saying hopefully and somewhat stupidly that marriage should be for life and a more realistic 36 per cent saying that it's perfectly reasonable these days for people to stay married for a while and move on.[2]

The mythical romantic passion inspired by grand views of marriage is so overpowering that almost half of people whose own marriages have failed still seem to believe that it was their fault, that they're anomalies in the great wed-for-life scheme, that they screwed it up somehow, that marriage should be forever but they couldn't pull it off. Personally I find this rather depressing – 49 per cent of people who've gone through a divorce still can't see that there's anything flawed in the beliefs and pressures attached to marriage. And as for these couples in first marriages and their cheesy romanticism, the same poll revealed that 18 per cent of husbands and 11 per cent of wives admitted to infidelities, with the numbers rising to 22 and 15 per cent respectively if you include those who refused to answer and probably have something to hide. So marriage is for life, but one does require a bit on the side to relieve the tedium? Interesting attitude.

According to Divorce UK, there were 160,000 divorces in England and Wales in 2002, an increase of almost 2 per cent from 2001.[3] The peak year for divorce in England and Wales was 2002, with 160,000; back in 1968, though, the rate was at about 50,000. The BBC says that the number of divorces in England and Wales dropped by 0.1 per cent in 2006 compared with 2003, but this correlates to the general drop in annual marriages.[4] The divorce rate remained the same, at 14 divorcing people per 1,000 of the married population. Of divorces in 2004, more than 69 per cent were granted to the wife.

In the United States, 1,163,000 divorces were granted in 2002. In 1997, 59 per cent of the US population was married, down from 62 per cent in 1990 and 72 per cent in 1970. Twenty-four per cent of the population had never married and 10 per cent was divorced, up from 8 per cent in 1990 and 6 per cent in 1980. Put these recent figures on a graph and the dramatic upswing becomes self-evident; and that's not even considering the massive changes that have occurred on the marital landscape since the sexual and gender revolution of the 1960s.

Bizarrely the divorce rate is significantly lower in blue states – those hotbeds of liberalism and amoral behaviour that traditionally vote Democrat – than in red states, where Republicans rule and neoconservative Christian values are generally upheld and respected. Christian and conservative Kentucky, Mississippi and Arkansas, all of which voted overwhelmingly to ban gay marriage, had three of the highest divorce rates in 2003 – 10.8, 11.1 and 12.7 per 1,000 members of the population respectively. The country's lowest rate was in Massachusetts, home of one-time presidential hopeful John Kerry, Democratic aristocracy the Kennedys and legal same-sex marriage, with 5.7 per 1,000 in 2003. Barbara Dafoe Whitehead, co-director of the National Marriage Project at Rutgers University, says, 'Some people are saying, "The Bible Belt is so pro-marriage, but gee, they have the highest divorce rates in the country." And there's a lot of worry in the red [republican] states about the high rate of divorce.'[5]

According to the Barna Group, a Californian organisation that studies evangelical Christian trends, 'Residents of the Northeast and West are commonly noted for their more liberal leanings in politics and lifestyle. However, the region of the nation in which divorce was least likely was the Northeast.'[6] So clearly religious belief is not stacking up the points in favour of couples staying together until God puts them asunder; so commonplace has divorce become that the very sectors of society who one would expect to be gritting their teeth and bearing anything for the sake of family values are the ones enjoying a mass exodus from marriage.

In Italy, meanwhile, there were 50,828 divorces in 2002, a 45 per cent increase from 2000. Three out of ten of these marriage break-ups are laid at the feet of interfering mothers-in-law and the unusually close relationship of Italian men to their mamas. According to psychologist Dr Annamaria Cassanese, disastrous in-laws fall into two categories – either they refuse to admit that they're ageing and see their sons' wives as competition, or they've devoted most of their lives to the family and they expect to get something back.[7] None of this is aided by the fact that Italian parents often help their newly married children buy apartments and cars, or the prevalence in Italy of *mammoni*, mothers' boys, sons who live at home with their parents well into their 30s, partly for economic reasons and partly because they enjoy being coddled. Cassanese says:

> In Italy there still exists a sort of mother love that is excessive. It is a very Latin thing, deeply embedded in our social structure. For example you will see mothers crying at the weddings of their sons, but they are not crying for joy, they are crying because they feel devastated. Their son has chosen another woman and it arouses very complex feelings, including jealousy.

So prevalent is the existence of *mammoni* that the Catholic Church's appeals court, the Sacra Rota, will actually grant an annulment to a woman who can prove that she's married to a mummy's boy, allowing both partners to remarry in a church should they choose to.

In Australia soaring divorce rates are fuelled by the baby boomer generation, whose men realise later in life that they don't have to stay in bad marriages. Unlike the depression generation, who slogged it out to the bitter end come hell or high water, boomers make their getaways when things get bad. Australians have the option of instigating divorce separately or together, and just under one-third of the 52,400 divorces granted in 2005 were joint applications. Fifty-seven per cent were instigated by the female partner, although men began to file for divorce more after the age of 50. Women are most dissatisfied with their marriages in the third and fourth year, when they comprise 63 per cent of single applications. After 30 years of marriage, though, 55 per cent of single applications are filed by men – there are a lot of women in their middle years being left by their husbands, a lot of younger men being left by their wives.[8] We don't know the social or personal effects of this trend but it's easy to speculate that first-wife syndrome is a cross many Australian women have to bear, as their wealthy and thus still marriageable spouses move on to pastures greener.

New Zealand experienced a sharp rise in its divorce rate in the early 1980s when the laws were changed to allow one partner to dissolve the marriage based on a two-year separation, far easier to prove than previous requirements.[9] After this sharp rise and a subsequent levelling out, the rates have been on a general increase since the late 1980s. Marriages in New Zealand don't last very long either – couples who were married for between five and nine years accounted for over 25 per cent of divorces in 1999. Almost two out of every five marriages dissolved that year had lasted for less than ten years.

In the United States, 82 per cent of married people stay together for five years. This drops to 52 per cent for 15 years, 20 per cent for 35 years and a lucky 5 per cent who make it to that golden 50-year mark. While the divorce rate in Japan is significantly lower than in the United States at a level of about half, it's almost doubled since 1990, with 264,000 couples formally breaking up in 2000.[10] The country's Health Ministry, meanwhile, estimates the numbers at just over 95,000 in 1970, rising to 206,955 in 1996. And this despite the highly unfavourable conditions for divorcing parents, whereby the one who leaves is not required to pay alimony or child support but will be permanently denied access to the child or children they leave behind. Tokyo divorce lawyer Hiroshi Shibuya explains, 'It's the Japanese general understanding that if they divorce, the noncustodial parent won't be able to see the kid again. It's as if the child loses a parent in an accident, as if that parent just dies.'[11]

Pravda newspaper estimates that a shocking 80 per cent of Russian marriages end in divorce, and the women involved have little chance of remarrying.[12] The mortality rate of working men is extremely high, women in their 30s significantly outnumber men and there just aren't enough blokes out there to get married to. Cuba's divorce rate, while difficult to specify, is known to be extremely high, with many Cubans marrying three or four times during their lives. Tellingly, though, divorce in Cuba is cheap – around $5 – and usually peaceful, a trend sociologists put down to the fact that separating Cubans don't generally have an awful lot of possessions to divide.

The sharp cost of splitting up

Couples all over the world are dissolving their marriages and walking away from mistakes and bad ideas with increasing ease. If there were any truth at all in the assumption that marriage equals commitment these spiralling figures would be halved, but instead it seems that more and more of us are entering into marriages with only the vaguest idea of why, and finding out after a few years that we really don't want to be there. Added to which, of course, is the fact that divorce really isn't cheap. It's difficult to estimate the cost of the whole excursion but it can be painfully steep. The BBC puts the total average price of a UK divorce at £13,000, around the standard for weddings,[13] while Sky News puts it an eye-watering £28,000 per couple, up from the lower figure to allow for increases in property prices.[14] It's possible to get a divorce for around £1,000, including solicitors' fees, £300 for the court proceedings and £40 for the decree absolute. That's assuming, however, that you have a completely amicable split with nothing contested and no property involved.

On the flip side is the fact that many UK couples, long married and with property, children and assets in common, actually can't afford to divorce. Soaring house prices make it almost impossible to go from paying for a single home to paying for two on the same salary, so if you want to leave the family home you may be forced to move into a small rented flat, or even worse, back in with your parents. Living as two is cheaper than living as one, so unless you're loaded, splitting into separate households is going to seriously tax your resources, both emotional and financial. Legal aid in divorce is tied to poverty so if you're not actually poor before the separation you won't get any help from the government – no matter how badly divorce can rock your economic position. This means that the partner with the less financial stability could feel forced to stay trapped in a horrible or abusive marriage rather than face the complete penury of being cut off from all assets.

Even if you are eligible for legal aid it can be a nightmare finding a solicitor; divorce is a huge money-spinner for the legal profession and there are fewer and fewer firms who take on low-paying work when they could making big bucks helping rich people screw their spouses out of everything they possibly can. The cost of the divorce itself is always paid by the couple – legal aid is only available to help you sort out issues around your children or your future finances. And if you do end up getting the house that counts as money you've earned, so you'll have to pay back the cost of the legal aid from that pot.

'There are a lot of middle-aged women who don't understand the legal system who contact us thinking their husbands will still provide, even in divorce,' says Christina Tait, founder of Divorce Aid, a voluntary group that helps people cope with the financial and emotional stress involved.[15] 'Then there are the men who are also stuck because, although their wives are entitled to legal aid, they have to pay legal fees out of their own pockets.' Insurers Alliance and Leicester say that divorcees spend more of their income paying off debt than any other group, which is a pleasant intimation of your future prospects, along with seeing your kids on alternate weekends and living in a grotty bedsit.

Divorce in the United Kingdom is big business. 'Divorce tourists' are even choosing to divest themselves of their wealthy spouses in the United Kingdom because there's a chance of a bigger payout. A recent study suggested that 8 January was the most popular day for Brits to file for divorce, with the pressures of Christmas and too much time cooped up with the family spurring record numbers of couples to finally call it quits. 'It is a bumper holiday season for family lawyers this year,' rejoiced a writer in the Law Society's *Law Gazette* in December 2005. 'Father Christmas has crammed his sack full of early presents.'[16] You have to wonder how he sleeps at night.

According to the *New York Sun*, in 2005 the average US divorce cost $50,000.[17] And it's not just the super-rich going divorce crazy – there's an entire industry starting up. Divorce party planners are the newest kids on the social block[18] and London has seen a boom in private investigators, most of whom find their information and make their money by 'blagging' – pretending to be from legitimate businesses that need to check account information as a way of finding out exactly what a spouse's hidden assets are.

Divorce lawyers get celebrity status for helping wealthy clientele suck the last possible drop of cashola out of their erring spouses. The kind of money at stake in these big name games can be astounding.

American Melissa Miller was 35 when her English husband Alan left her for another woman. So far, so sad but standard. The difference, though, is that Alan is a high-flying multi-millionaire fund manager who's worth a fortune and Melissa had given up her well-paying job when they married. The marriage lasted less than three years and they had no children, but when she took him to court the lucky Ms Miller was awarded a whopping £5 million. It's nowhere near as much as some of the bigger payouts – of which more in a moment – but those went to wives who'd been married for decades. In this case, Melissa was a smart young professional who'd made £85,000 a year before her marriage, had only been out of her job for three years and could probably have climbed her way back up the ladder fairly quickly. But with a £2.3 million house in Chelsea and a £2.7 lump sum payout filling the gap left by her husband's little indiscretion, she probably doesn't need to.

Miller's lawyer was outraged, calling the settlement a 'meal ticket for life'. The judge in the case, however, disagreed, saying Melissa had married her fund manager with a 'reasonable expectation' of a certain type of (insanely wealthy) lifestyle that had now been taken away due to her husband's infidelity. Rich men across the country shuddered in their chauffeur-driven Bentleys when news of the Miller settlement broke, and a whole new generation of perfectly manicured trophy wives was born.

Notable mostly for setting a new and terrifying precedent, Melissa's lottery ticket pales in comparison with some of the more excessive divorce windfalls of recent years. Self-confessed sex addict Michael Douglas paid his wife Diandra $45 million to be released from their marriage and into the welcoming arms of Welsh crumpet Catherine Zeta-Jones (who reportedly made sure she'd be covered if he went back to his old ways by inserting a massive 'you stray, you pay' clause into their pre-nup). Brit Stephen Marks, who founded the French Connection clothing store, sold £40 million worth of shares in the company to pay his ex-wife Alisa's settlement, rumoured to be around £50 million. Craig McCaw met wife Wendy when she tutored him at Stanford University in 1974. Twenty-six years later the cable television heir paid out more than $460 million to his now ex-wife, mostly in stocks.

When Saudi businessman Adnan Khashoggi split from jet-setting wife Soraya, she walked away with around $874 million in an out-of-court settlement. Russian billionaire Roman Abramovich paid his former air hostess wife Irina what's believed to be the biggest settlement ever, somewhere in the region of $2.5 billion, when he was caught cheating with a much younger mistress and his presidential pal Vladimir Putin allegedly told him to clean up his act. Media baron Rupert Murdoch had three children with Anna, his wife of 32 years, and their split became far from amicable when he tried to force her off the board of his global empire Newscorp. By the time the divorce was finalised in 1999 she got an astonishing $1.7 billion, including $110 million in cash. It would almost be worth being married to Rupert Murdoch for that kind of money.

A case history and a home in pieces

It might not be billions, but the little people are getting stiffed by Divorce Inc too. Richard, 34, fell hard for a Canadian woman he met online and decided to make a go of things with her. But his romantic gesture has resulted in a legal and possibly financial nightmare. He says:

> She came over to the UK three times at my expense over the course of a year, and the fourth time she entered the country on a marriage and settlement visa. We got married soon after (the visa and wedding were paid for by me and family) but the marriage was a disaster, and she left me three months later. She

> was arrogant, stubborn and racist. Her behaviour was extreme, and there was the constant threat of 'if you don't do what I want I'll leave you and go back to Canada'. The whole experience cost me around £10,000. I now know she had done this before to other men, including her first husband, who was Scottish and the father of her eldest child. She has a second child by a different father. Fortunately she didn't get pregnant by me.

And that should have been the end of that, but it wasn't. Richard continues:

> A year after our marriage I commenced divorce proceedings and papers were served on her in Canada, but she didn't return them. I signed an affidavit to state that I had spoken to her on the phone and that she had said she had received the papers. But the Court wants further proof of service and she seems to have disappeared. She's doing this purely to spite me as she is a very nasty piece of work. My current partner and I bought a house about a year ago after I'd served papers on my ex, but I'm terrified I may lose everything we've worked for, including part of my pension, to a woman who is basically a con artist, who lives off others and the state. She never had any money of her own when she came to this country nor did a day's work in it. I feel totally despairing that I will ever be rid of her or able to live my life without this shadow hanging over me. All this for a sham marriage which lasted 13 weeks!

Divorce courts are tough places. When it comes to separating assets they often take a hard line that doesn't consider the complainants' emotional connections to their possessions. Why should they? If you've got to the stage where you hate each other so much that you can't come to some arrangement yourselves, then you each obviously want to get as much as you can out of the other and it's all about money. That's what happened to Dr Nicholas Bartha, one of the more tragic divorce tales of recent years.

Romanian Bartha was married to a Dutch woman, Cordula Hahn. Their marriage was, by all accounts, extremely strange, although it produced two daughters. Hahn filed for divorce in 2001 after removing herself and her daughters to a small apartment. Her husband was ordered to pay her a hefty settlement – a settlement that would have entailed selling his house. Whether Bartha was cold and emotionally abusive or not, whether he mistreated her or not, whether he was, in fact, slightly insane or not, everyone involved agreed that he loved his house with an uncommon passion. For an immigrant to the United States to own a historic $5 million town house between Park and Madison Avenues in New York was an unquestionable sign of success, of having arrived, of living the American dream. And Bartha was *very* attached to that dream. In April 2005 Hahn received a court-ordered settlement of $4 million and a property credit; there was no way around it, he would have to sell the house. But Bartha didn't want to sell, he wanted to stay there for the rest of his life. And like most determined men Bartha got what he wanted.

In July 2006 the graceful home on East 62nd street was levelled by a vicious gas explosion. Charred and barely recognisable, Bartha was pulled from the rubble. A day later he died from burns to 35 per cent of his body, with the New York coroner calling it suicide. When the smoke cleared an email was released that he'd sent both to Hahn and to various news outlets around the city. In amongst the enraged suicidal rambling was the following heart-wrenching statement: 'You will be transformed from gold digger to ash and rubbish digger. You always wanted me to sell the house and I always told you "I will leave the house only if I am dead." You ridiculed me. You should have taken it seriously.' Would Bartha still be alive if divorce courts hadn't forced him to face the threat of losing his home? We'll never know, but what we do know is that the financial burden of a settlement payout had a far more human cost than expected. And this is why it's not wise to leave our emotional well-being in the hands of a legal system that has no room for the spiritual, the personal, the complex, the grey area, because its chief concern is money.[19]

Divorce seems to bring out the worst in people. Where once a couple cared enough about each other to want to be together forever, put them in a divorce court and they turn into frantic grasping harpies with no relation to logic or reason or kindness. I spoke to an English family lawyer who had tales that would turn a lesser person off marriage for life. She told me of one case where, after a very long and acrimonious divorce, the judge ordered the husband to leave the local authority house the couple had shared and transfer the tenancy to the wife. A lot of hard work and various threats of court action ensured that he eventually did. The wife then decided that she did not want to stay in the house because her husband was harassing her, so she arranged a house swap. On moving day, the husband turned up with his van and took away the patio stone by stone. As he said, 'I laid it, I paid for it and it's my patio, and I'm not leaving it for anyone else.'

Another couple this lawyer acted for managed to agree how to divide about £230,000 in assets, fix on child maintenance, and run up a bill in excess of £30,000 each in legal fees, but then spent four hours in the lobby of the court (with a barrister and a solicitor apiece) arguing about a blue glass vase and a print of Tuscany. Those four hours probably cost each of them £2,000.

A third couple had been married for 27 years, but spent the last nine years in the same house without saying one word to each other. The wife finally plucked up the courage to divorce the husband and then was upset that he didn't say anything. And one husband demanded to be reimbursed for cat food he'd paid for during the 22-year marriage on the basis that he never wanted the bloody cat anyway.

Any relationship break-up can be painful, traumatic and expensive, and being part of a couple means running the risk of splitting up in a way that's less than ideal. But your average break-up doesn't have to involve courts, lawyers and costs, a nightmare that often ramps up the level of acrimony to 11. Divorce in the United Kingdom costs around £4.3 billion a year; $175 billion is spent on divorce a year in the United States, mostly on litigation.[20] Homes are lost, families go into debt, prospects are destroyed every day. The numbers speak for themselves, but I'll spell it out for you if I have to. How do you avoid going through a messy divorce that wrecks your financial health for life? It's so simple it almost hurts. *Don't get married.*

Some emotional consequences

It's not like we're gaining any life-changing self-knowledge from these painful and expensive encounters. According to Christine Northam of the UK's public family counselling service Relate:

> Second marriages break up almost twice as often as first marriages. I've been at Relate since 1995 and I've seen an awful lot. People don't learn their lessons, that's why second marriages fail so often. It's very hopeful when a couple comes in for counselling because it means they're ready and willing to try and understand what's happening to them. It's so easy to just blame your previous partner; we help people examine their first marriages, understand where they were to blame in what went wrong. That's the counselling process – finding out what part they played in the break-up and why they chose to be with who they choose to be with. It's an exhilarating process to be part of

> because it really takes courage. Understanding yourself is the most important thing; it makes a huge contribution to personal happiness.[21]

Not understanding yourself, on the other hand, can lead to the kind of angst-laden divorce drama without which Jerry Springer would be working at Burger King.

We've all heard horrible divorce stories; we probably all know someone who's been screwed by their former spouse for money, or property, or just time with the kids. I can't think of many people who joyfully talk about what a fabulous experience their divorce was, no matter how pleased they are to be out of their marriages. But awful divorces being as common as they are doesn't make them any less painful or damaging when it's you involved.

The blow can come anywhere, even to people who seem the most secure, the most stable. Susan, from Idaho, is in her late 40s and dealing with the fallout from a divorce that shocked her completely. She explains, 'On the day my youngest child moved into the dorm at college, my husband of 23 years told me he wanted a divorce, saying he'd been terribly unhappy the whole time and that I contributed nothing to the marriage. Never mind that I raised three kids within two and a half years and worked full time while his job required long hours and much out-of-town time. He said he "had" to drink because of me, had to be on depression medication because of me, he always knew he would some day have to leave me and he just tried not to think about it, it was all my fault, and even though he never said a word to me about his unhappiness I just should have known.

'I later found out that he jokingly told family members and friends a couple of years ago he was going to leave when the kids got out of school and had often made mean comments behind my back. For the last few years I'd felt very distant from him – we never went anywhere or did anything together, I felt like a stranger getting into the car with him. He had lost his job of 20 years and I thought he was depressed because of this. There was another woman – again, he said, it was my fault. He said that I'd caused him to be what he is today.

'I've tried to act maturely, not to lash back in anger, to let him know I care, to be willing to address my part in it, but he's refused to speak to me or have any contact with me ever since, even to the point of sending me any necessary mail without putting his return address or even his name. In the year since he left he has never called our house, even to talk to his children. He emails them on the few occasions he wants to see them and meets them out for dinner. They do not know where he lives. He has almost totally erased us from his life and is currently attempting to force us to sell our home and move into a condo. I am lost. My children are all in college. My household is moving from a very busy five to just me. I've felt totally powerless and voiceless in all of this.'

Susan's is not a wildly uncommon case. Abandoned by someone she thought she'd built a life with, she's left to flounder along somehow with only the dregs of that existence to prop her up. She sank everything she had into her marriage, all her emotional resources, all her time, all her energy, and it took only her husband's mid-life crisis or slide into depression or innate nastiness or whatever was to blame for his behaviour to completely destabilise her world. This is one of the risks you take when you put all your eggs in one basket and subsume yourself into your marriage (or indeed any relationship). When all your happiness rests on the actions of a single pivotal person and you have no real life outside of them, you will always be facing the possibility that they can leave. They can go, and you will be alone, and no matter how hard you've worked or how much love you've given them you will wind up with nothing.

Hash Varsani is 33, an Anglo-Indian photographer and designer who split up with his wife a few years ago. He's eloquent and funny, has a wise and philosophic attitude to his painful divorce, and has made sure to learn a few important lessons from its less salubrious consequences.

He says, 'I met Stephanie when I was on a photographic trip. I was taken aback because no one had given me that much attention in a very long time. I got this unique opportunity to go to Canada, and I came home with a girlfriend.

'My parents are from Gujarat, first generation, and were trying to mould me into being part of the Indian community away from India. I even had four prospective brides chosen for me. I went along with it for a while but then things started getting serious with Steph so I made a decision and said right, I need to leave. Dad, me and you are fighting too much. I became the ostracised eldest son who wasn't talking to anyone.

'Steph came over to England and six months later I proposed. I was 26 and that was my first ever independent manoeuvre. My parents never came to the wedding, my uncle gave me away. We had two weddings and they were both beautiful. We had the most amazing time that summer but then it kind of went downhill.

'She didn't understand that I gave up a lot of things to be with her. She had no passion, no ambition, lacked confidence as well, and that instilled a lot of friction in our relationship. We stopped communicating about the bigger picture. We never spoke about children. I had dreams of going to Thailand, maybe settling down in Italy or Paris, just travelling. All she wanted to do was go home. For me that was boring as fuck, because there's nothing to do on that farm outside Toronto.

'We had arguments, we'd fight, we lost our intimacy for the last two years of that three-year marriage. I hung around my friends, organising events, doing photography, introducing myself to a much larger group of people. I was the boisterous, outgoing, big-laughing person that wants to meet people. She felt so out of sync. She had never realised who I was.

'She was the wrong person for me – wrong shape, wrong height, wrong character. I did love her but when I suddenly noted that I was doing everything for the wrong reason I started to become very selfish. If you cannot move a relationship forward with that person and enhance it over your lifetime it's not going to work. Because I was too young to appreciate that, I took it really, really hard when the relationship ended.

'We finally broke down when she got an intimate text message from another man on a Saturday morning. She was in the shower so I read it, because the trust had completely gone. We fought about it all weekend. She didn't admit anything but I was breaking things, doors and windows and the classic smashing of glasses and all that. It was my house, so eventually I made her leave.

'We had a joint account that more or less broke my bank. I got left the house on the condition that when I sold it I would give her half the net. She started asking me for things that were highly disagreeable, in a court of law. She'd walk in when I was out and take things. The bed – that was a very contentious issue. The TV, the sound system, my glass table, the sofa, the television that my father had given me . . . all of these things that were effectively my possessions were being removed from my house.

'After it finished I threw myself into work and women. I slept with a client and four other people in the space of two weeks. I nailed some massive contracts, just being a media whore. It was making me feel good but I didn't care enough about the people I was sleeping with. Then I started drinking and losing clients. I wasn't earning any money, I couldn't pay the mortgage, I lost the car because I was drink driving, got sent to prison for three weeks. That was the bottom of my curve. I learnt a lot from that. It gave me time to think and to recover.

'I won't get married again. It's a case of been there, done that. The divorce was so destructive. Now if I was with someone I really loved I'd want some way to mark our commitment, but nothing legal or official. I don't think it's the world's business how I conduct my relationships. It's private and it will stay that way.'

It felt so nice I did it twice

If marriage was as commitment-tastic as the blind and/or romantic among us would like to believe there wouldn't be the rash of multiple-marital mania that's putting fortunes in the pockets of therapists, divorce courts and wedding planners across the developed world. Samuel Johnson, the 18th-century writer and essayist, called second marriages 'the triumph of hope over experience'. Lord only knows what he would have thought about third marriages. Or seventh marriages.

The four-marriage club includes William Shatner, Yoko Ono, Lisa Marie Presley, Muhammad Ali, James Brown, Frank Sinatra and Peter Sellers. What a bunch of minimalists. If you're going to do it, why not go for five? Billy Bob Thornton did. So did Joan Collins (despite insisting that she needed 'a wife, not a husband'), Judy Garland, Geena Davis, Henry Fonda and Dennis Hopper. Rock and roll pioneer Jerry Lee Lewis: six wives, including his adorable first cousin (twice removed) Myra Gale Brown, then just 13 years old and still a believer in Santa Claus.[22] Singer/songwriter Greg Allmann: six wives, including the inimitable Cher. Hollywood producer and all-around bad boy Robert Evans: seven wives, a parade of pulchritude and some astonishing alimony payments. Talk show host Larry King: seven marriages, two of them to the same former

Playboy Bunny. Actor Mickey Rooney: eight wives, the shortest for 100 days, the longest for 22 years. Now that's variation for you. Blonde bombshell Lana Turner: eight marriages, two to restaurateur Steven Crane. Elizabeth Taylor, lover of big rocks and one of the 20th century's most celebrated beauties: eight marriages, two of them to her *Cleopatra* co-star Richard Burton. She's currently single, although it took a long time to learn that particular lesson. (She once said, 'I am a very committed wife. And I should be committed too – for being married so many times.') Zsa Zsa Gabor: nine husbands – a diplomat, hotelier Conrad Hilton, an actor, a CEO, an oilman, an inventor, the divorce lawyer from her previous marriage, a playboy and a prince, to whom she's still married. At the time of writing. God only knows what could have happened in the interim.[23] After all, we're talking about the woman who came up with this gem of an aphorism: 'I am a wonderful housekeeper. I get divorced, I keep the house.'

And like just about every other example in this book, where Hollywood's best and brightest lead the rest of us will surely follow. Former police officer Kamarudin Mohamad made headlines in 2004 when he became Malaysia's most married man, remarrying his first ever wife Khadijah Udin, whom he divorced almost 50 years before after just one year. It was his 53rd marriage. The others lasted an average of 193 days each.[24] According to *The Guinness Book of World Records*, Baptist Minister Glynn 'Scotty' Wolfe, of Blythe, California, has had the most number of monogamous marriages.[25] His 29th and final marriage was a publicity stunt for a UK TV documentary. He married Linda Essex, of Anderson, Indiana, herself wed a rather unusual 23 times. According to Wolfe's son his father was 'picky and stubborn and against living in sin'. So obviously, when his wife pissed him off the only logical solution was to divorce her and get another one who'd be less trouble.

These are stories of excess but they help highlight the transience of marriage and how little effect that ceremony, piece of paper and really expensive cake need have on the lifespan of your relationship. If you aren't going to stick it out you aren't going to stick it out, unless you're forced to because you can't afford to get divorced, which is a prospect that should be enough to put most of us off for life.

I'm not suggesting that people are inherently cynical – people other than me, that is – and that they get married without expecting it to last. On the contrary, it seems that many of us enter into marriage, no matter how many times we've done it before, with our eyes shut tight and our fists clenched, muttering, 'This is it, this is the one, I just know it is,' only to be faced with an unpleasant surprise once the short sharp shock of mutual delusion has worn off. And then we're left floundering to collect the shattered fragments of our self-esteem and our belief in forever, only to go away, forget most of what happened, blame our former spouse for not being Cinderella or Prince Charming and then charge headlong back into the same situation without learning a damned thing. Sure, in a way I suppose it's romantic, this unshakeable belief in the enduring power of love despite all evidence to the contrary. Believing you can fly is also romantic in its way, until it talks you up to the top of a very high building.

Maya's tale is unusual, but both entertaining and cautionary. She's 30 and has two children, is highly educated, previously of private means. She's been married five – yes, *five* – times, and is still with her fifth husband (although, tellingly, she refers to him as 'current'). 'I fell passionately in love with a 17-year-old soldier when I was 12,' she says, 'and we dated until I was 15. We broke up when my parents and I moved. I was heartbroken and didn't have any other serious relationships until I started marrying them. After that I married them all.

'The first one was the day after my 18th birthday. We were only together for three days before he proposed. I was wankered for about a month and when I sobered up I was married to a total stranger.[26] I thought, who the bloody hell is this man in my house? I don't even remember the wedding. I was in my lawyer's office 48 hours later trying to make it all go away. We got it annulled eventually but it was painful both financially and emotionally. It cost me £60,000 to get rid of him, and he's still belligerent and shitty every time I see him. At the time I was working on TV and he decided to sell the entire story to a tabloid Sunday paper. I was completely humiliated and embarrassed.

'My second wedding was six months later, when I was still 18. We wanted to live together and because of his job we had to be married. Everyone tried to talk me out of it. We had a great wedding, though I spent time mostly with my family and friends, not the groom. The party cost £24,000 – my dress alone was £9,000 – but it was worth it. That was all that was good about it, though. He beat the living crap out of me after we were married, broke my nose, jaw, four ribs, arm, femur, even tried to strangle me and threw me out a window. I wound up with a broken pelvis, a fractured spine and skull and a broken wrist. I was pregnant with twins and I lost them. Our divorce was done by legal aid. Everyone around me was furious because of what he'd done. My daughter, who I'd had before we were married, was totally traumatised by the relationship, and the divorce kickstarted her recovery.

'By the time of my third wedding my family were like, "Oh God, another one! Not again!" Fair view, I guess. I was 21 by then and I married him because it fulfilled the expected life pattern. I caught him shagging one of my mates and that was it for us, although my friends and family were actually pretty hostile; they thought I should have forgiven him his first "indiscretion".

It ended up costing me £15,000 to get out of it but there was no emotional cost, and my daughter wasn't really bothered.

'Marriage number four was a lot worse. I was 24 and again I married him because it seemed like the appropriate thing to do. By the time it finally ended we hadn't had sex for three years. I worked a 70-hour week, we slept in different rooms, we had a massive argument in 2001 that basically carried on until 2004, but he still couldn't figure out why I left him. The last time we had sex I was comatose on Valium and didn't even realise I was being fucked. The final straw was when I caught him shagging my best mate on our living-room floor. I never told him I saw them at it, even though he brought her to court with him during divorce proceedings.

'Everyone acted like it was my fault. They all went "I told you so" and "People don't change". The first time I went back to the marital home to drop the kids off after we split, my best friend of 20 years was sat in the living-room wearing my slippers and dressing gown and playing Lady Muck. I said, "You may be shagging my husband, you may be living in my house and driving my Porsche Boxster, you may be wearing my clothes and living my life, but get your fucking feet off my sofa." It worked – she got her feet off.

'I lost everything in that one – home, company, my personal belongings. The only things I kept were my two sports cars. I was supposed to get a £400,000 payout but he fucked off to a country that's not a signatory to the Geneva Convention so I couldn't get him to pay up. He tried to take our son with him but luckily I found out the day before and got an emergency prohibitive order to withdraw his passport. My barristers were shockingly bad from an asset division perspective but fab at making sure my son couldn't leave the UK.

'Both my kids were heartbroken. After years of trying to adopt my daughter he dropped her as if she was a hot potato.

At first he used to have both kids for half the week, but it didn't work. My son is autistic and has ADHD and his father used to forget his medication all the time. Even the school expressed concern at how neglected he was. When I called a halt to it he got on a plane and left the country. Our son doesn't understand why his dad has so little to do with him, so he gets sad and angry. Two Christmases ago my ex-husband arranged to have them both on Boxing Day, they were ready and so excited, waiting in the garden for him to turn up. When he arrived he took only his son and told my daughter that he needed time with his "real kids". I will never forgive him for this.

'I married my fifth husband for the completely fucked up reason of actually being in love. My first four weddings were all in registry offices: this one was in a church, full service with the older vows. I paid for everything myself because my hubby is a tight-fisted git. When I walked into the church I just wanted to turn around and run away, but I couldn't because 250 people were looking at me. I only knew about 40 of them.

'My dress didn't fit, I got to the church too early, I was so nervous that I was swearing under my breath and everyone heard me, my husband-to-be didn't even bother to turn around and look at me, I got my shoes caught in all three heating grates and ended up having to leave them in the aisle, the priest mucked up my name and my boobs fell out of my dress when I was signing the register. The only saving graces were that my son didn't eat the rings and my daughter did the most beautiful reading. The reception was horrible too, all the speeches took the piss out of me, including a warning about wedding number six. My husband didn't stand up for me at all.

'My husband changed a lot after we got married. He treats me as his property, talks to me as if I'm five and no longer makes any effort. We both work but I pay all the household expenses and also do all the cooking and cleaning. I feel like a slave who's paying for the privilege. Things are physically better – he doesn't beat me – but on an emotional level they're much, much worse. I ask him for a kiss and he pulls faces. I don't feel looked after or protected. If I ask for sex more than once a fortnight he responds like I'm a crazed nymphomaniac pervert.

'I think my history indicates I could get married again. And while I don't want to and can't imagine getting divorced, if things go tits up then I know I'll do both again. I've learnt that every question has three basic answers. If things aren't perfect you can either bail out, brush it aside and carry on with a clean slate or carry on without forgiving or forgetting, and if you want it to last you have to work on it later with no reservations. I've also learnt not to worry, because what's the point?

'Love is not the "be all and end all", it cannot conquer all, only hope and effort can do that. I've learnt that you should protect your assets even when blinded by emotions. Never make a decision based purely on your heart or your head, you have to have a mix of both. A good marriage takes effort from both parties.'

Commitment without marriage

So no, getting married does not mean that you're committed. It may mean that you'd *like* to be committed, or that commitment is an ideal you hold dear, but blowing thousands and getting all your friends to watch is not a surefire way to make those romantic dreams come true. Not getting married, in fact, can be just as certain a path to sticking it out for the long term. Sim, 34 (we met her in Chapter Five too), is completely secure in her relationship with Tom. She explains it well:

> We haven't lost a single thing from not getting married because it would not change our relationship in any way. We are

> committed to each other and do not need society's legal document or to announce our commitment in front of others to feel more secure in our relationship. Marriage does not seem more romantic but less so to me, because Tom and I are not legally bound but choose to be together every day. It may be many girls' dreams to one day walk down the aisle and it's good that they live that dream, but it was never mine. Other than living out the daydream I can't really see the argument for marriage. People have told me that I'm not showing commitment to Tom until I marry him but you can leave your husband just like you can leave your boyfriend, as almost 50 per cent of the married British population have shown. Ultimately our relationship and feelings for each other are about the two of us and nobody else, and that's one of the things I love about it. I feel bound to Tom by something far stronger than a marriage document could ever show.

The idea that only marriage signifies commitment is deeply offensive to couples the world over who've had serious, fruitful, meaningful long-term relationships. It's still impossible in most countries for same-sex couples to get married or cement their unions in any formal way but that's never stopped gay people from staying together for the long haul. The creation of civil partnerships – which is not, by the way, quite the same as 'gay marriage', marriage still being defined on the rule books as a union between a man and a woman – is without a doubt an important step for the legislation of equality, but there's a downside to this apparent triumph too. If straight people can blow their savings on ridiculous weddings, suffer through painful divorces and be pressured into getting married instead of being able to dictate the terms of their own relationships, then why shouldn't gay people? They want equality, we'll give them equality – down to the misery, the angst and the heartbreak! That'll learn 'em.

When South Africa legalised same-sex partnerships in 2006 the response was overwhelmingly positive, mainly because it seemed to be a step towards bringing homosexuality out of Africa's closet. In a country that neighbours Robert Mugabe's Zimbabwe, where being openly gay could get you killed, it was a crucial move in the legitimisation of homosexual rights and in admitting that gay people exist, are part of society, contribute. But not everyone was overwhelmingly pleased, with some members of the gay community less than thrilled that they'd now be expected to act like their conformist heterosexual peers. Midi Achmat, a 42-year-old finance professional and vocal gay rights campaigner in the Western Cape, has been with her partner for 21 years.[27] She says, 'I would not get married. I am not interested – I don't want to follow rules that straight people do. South Africa's divorce rate is one of the highest in the world, so let's hope the change in law does not add to it. My partner and I have a commitment to each other but that is not seen as a marriage because we are gay, because we are lesbian.'[28]

I'm not suggesting that legislating for gay people to have rights equal to straight people is in any way a bad thing. Of course not, but maybe creating a situation where gay people are placed under exactly the same pressures as straight people is not quite the answer. It's the homogenisation solution so beloved of politicians raising its ugly head again – 'If we make everybody exactly the same then we won't have to remember so many annoying little details.' 'Brilliant, Giles! Write it into the law books.'

Journalist Catherine Bennett wrote in the *Guardian*:

> Apart from the occasional presence of religious fanatics with placards, the most remarkable thing about the civil partnership ceremonials reported so far has, surely, been their resemblance

> to the established heterosexual model . . . [embracing] down to the smallest, most grotesque detail, the conventions of the standard wedding.[29]

And she's right – 'pink' wedding companies have sprung up across the United Kingdom as gay couples clamour to do everything exactly the way straight couples do, just better and with organic cake. And that's not all that's being adopted in this cross-orientation pollination. Soon after the law came into being in the United Kingdom an article from *Legal Week* said, 'The new law carries with it significant opportunities for the private client legal market to target those same-sex partners whose interest has been engaged by the new law and bring them into the office for advice.'[30] Which means that, just like hetero couples, they might want to think about getting a 'pre-registration agreement' in case they later need 'a framework for an elegant disengagement in the event of a dissolution of the civil partnership'. Oh joy – gay people can have prenups and divorces too (although as anyone who's been through it will tell you, they're rarely elegant).

I don't pretend to have a convenient alternative solution to this dilemma and there's a good chance that the civil partnership situation may turn out to be a winner for everyone, which would be lovely. There's an equally good chance, though, that ten years down the line same-sex couples will be hassling their partners, 'If you really loved me you'd marry me,' and mothers across the country will be asking their sons when they're going to make an honest man of young James because he does seem so nice. And then the upshot, along with the pleasant legal consequences of being able to leave things to your partner when you die, will be a whole new swathe of couples in therapy, in recovery and in the divorce courts.

'Gay marriage' in France has taken a very different turn from this twee cakes 'n' cash English tendency, to the point where heterosexual couples are choosing to enter into civil partnerships rather than full-on marriages. The highest-profile example of this is probably 31-year-old author Mazarine Pingeot, the illegitimate daughter of former president Francois Mitterrand who was kept in hiding for the 14 years of her father's presidency for fear of the public reaction. She decided on a civil partnership rather than marriage with Moroccan filmmaker Muhamad Ulan-Mohand, the father of her son Astor.

Le Pacte Civil de Solidarité (Civil Solidarity Pact), known as *le Pacs*, was created in 1999 after a long campaign by gay and lesbian groups and confers rights in areas like taxes, social security and housing. But the number of heterosexual couples going for this option has confounded expectations – according to Patrick Festy, a researcher at the French National Institute of Demographic Studies, 85 per cent of people committing to civil pacts are heterosexual. 'The pact is open to heterosexual couples but when it was launched I didn't think it offered them anything,' says Maître Véronique Frances-Virtel, a notary in eastern France. 'Now, with hindsight, I realise that it fulfilled a need for heterosexual couples who live together but who don't want to get married. I see people who were traumatised by their parents' divorce and have been put off marriage as a result, or who are divorced themselves. When they enter into a new relationship, some don't want to remarry for the sake of their children. For all those people – as well as for those who are ideologically opposed to marriage – *le Pacs* can be a solution.'[31] It seems a cunning resolution to the problem of marriage, allowing people a painless, convenient and beneficial way to share their property and responsibilities without tying them into the chokehold that the 'traditional' institution imposes.

Some couples, of course, don't even require that technicality to confirm their commitment, capable as they are of believing in their own choices without bureaucratic attention. Bob is 53, Scottish, and has been with his lover for 23 years. A stage actor, he turned his back on his career when his partner fell ill and he needed more job stability to make sure the bills were paid. They'd been living together for 18 years by then. Giving up your vocation so you can provide for your lover in their time of need sounds an awful lot like commitment, doesn't it? And despite the new availability of civil partnership for same-sex couples in the United Kingdom they have no intention of dashing off the nearest pink-draped altar, for reasons both personal and political.

Bob says, 'I wouldn't have married my first "husband", even if it was an option. We were very politicised then, in the late 70s, very left wing – marriage was passé for our generation. We didn't recognise the need to legitimise our relationship by going through a legal or religious process. Homosexuality was still illegal in Scotland at the time so it was an impossibility anyway. You faced life imprisonment. No was ever charged, mind you, but it was strictly illegal. It was made legal in England in 1968 but legalisation in Scotland followed in the late 70s. Things in this country move terribly slowly. That's one reason why the gay community then was politically active, far more than they are today. We were committed politically to a whole lot of causes. That whole generation of student strikes, after 1968 and Paris, it fed through to the late 70s. But Thatcher put a stop to that, she just oozed repression.

'This was about when we started to say, hang on, gay people pay taxes, we contribute to society, we have rights. There were cases of people living together for 30, 40 years and one partner died and the deceased's relatives would take everything. Lots of people didn't write wills – most of us didn't have a great deal to leave. But the families would deny your right to attend your partner's funeral. Absolutely shocking. There have been huge changes for the better, but at the same time there's a hell of a lot of work to do and not that many people out there agit-propping. There's Elton John getting married, which is all very nice, but I'm a total cynic – I firmly believe the civil partnerships bill was totally financially driven.

'My partner and I have been together for 24 years this summer and when we come to retire, which isn't that long away, we will both get individual pensions, which will amount to a hell of a lot more than a married pension. So all these gay men and women who are getting married now will eventually be getting one pension. And that's not broadcast – I don't think they realise. The only credits you really get for being married are if you have a string of kids.

'I wouldn't want to do it now at any rate. I've survived 23 years with my partner without having to cement it any more. I've never felt the need for a big party or ceremony. I think it would embarrass me in a peculiar way because I don't believe in it, I don't believe in marriage as an institution, I wouldn't compromise my principles for it. I've been a born and bred atheist all my life and marriage started off as a religious thing. I think people want to couple and stay together for life if the relationship remains viable; but if it doesn't remain viable then they should be able to say kiss goodbye and let's get on with it. All marriage does is make divorce lawyers very, very rich. The divorce rate is rising every year. I don't see what benefit cementing yourself to a legal contract – I mean, that's all it is – has.'

If your relationship is strong and healthy and you choose to be in it every day it shouldn't need to be legitimised by a piece of paper. The assumption that marriage means you're committed suggests that you couldn't imagine being committed *without* marriage. And if your attachment to your partner won't stand up all by itself then no ceremony is going to bind you together. Marriage does not work magic; no matter how many bridesmaids you rope in, no matter how many cover bands you hire to play Wet Wet Wet songs for your first dance, no matter how much of a thrill you get from using someone else's surname, the only things that will keep a couple together are luck, care and a lot of hard work.

CONCLUSION

There are some wonderful marriages out there. Some couples have the good fortune, tolerance, patience, temperance and tenacity to make it work, which is fantastic for them. I respect and admire their situations. I also respect and admire primary school teachers, but that doesn't make me suited to controlling a room full of eight-year-olds. There's no question that good marriages happen and that they work to the benefit of everyone involved; I'm not disputing that. What I am disputing is the universality of the institution, the assumption that we all have to do it, that no other relationship or lifestyle marks us out as adult and functional members of society. Avoiding marriage, for whatever reason, is often seen as antisocial, immature, even just weird. But the plain fact is that marriage isn't for everyone and those of us who aren't sure about it, who feel pulls in different directions, who are having too much fun to settle down, shouldn't be bullied and bribed into a lifetime commitment that we don't really want.

This book has dealt, in the main, with extreme situations: nightmare couplings, disastrous divorces, errors on an epic scale. Of course not everyone will face this kind of torment in their lives, of course not every marriage will end like this, and of course relationships of any stripe face many of the same difficulties as marriages. But I've used these cautionary tales to make a point, to illustrate the consequences of bad choices taken to unpleasant conclusions; and trust me, it gets a lot worse than this.

As a general rule, none of the reasons I was given by my respondents stood up to close scrutiny. Those with happy marriages usually didn't bother to give much explanation of why they'd tied the knot because to them it was a natural, obvious step to take. They'd say things like 'It just seemed right' or 'We were ready' or even 'I don't know, do you know? Why *did* we get married?' followed by some adorable coupley bickering. It was the ones with the failed attempts or the horror stories who scrabbled around desperately trying to come up with concrete and convincing motivations, and they were the ones who had suffered the worst effects.

I chose to arrange this book by reasons because so many of the people I encountered were bitter and angry with themselves for not thinking more carefully, for assuming that because they had what appeared to be a common and concrete cause for marriage there was no need for them to interrogate that impulse. If the window dressing for marriage seemed right they jumped right into it, because *that's what you do*.

Let's think about those motivations again. You married for love? Love is fleeting and transient, and it's not just me saying that, it's chemistry. Many of the emotions you think you feel may well just be hormones, your body's in-built urge to procreate talking your mind into believing there's something unique and quintessential about the person you're attracted to other than their appealing genetic make-up. These hormones fade, and what do they leave behind them? Consequences, complications, commitments. Added to that is the fact that until the last two centuries love was deemed inappropriate within marriage, which was a practical and not an emotional partnership. The two-person coupling comes from physical, economic and political necessity, not from a desire to skip through the flowers together. The commonly held belief that marriage has always been about two people who are deeply in love setting sail on the sea of life together is patently untrue.

You married for financial or legal reasons? Not only are those benefits far smaller than they're made out to be, you've discounted all the other effects of marriage. Your spouse, yourself, your parents or friends or society at large may take that commitment more seriously than you do and may alter how they relate to you in response. Not to mention the fact that you could be committing a very serious offence that has greater repercussions than the emotional.

You wanted a wedding? Parties are all well and good but they have costs less obvious than the price of the caterer. It's all too easy to be yet another mindless polluting consumer contributing to the slow death of the planet, especially when you have an enormous event to put on and sustainability is the last thing on your mind. And then there are the financial penalties, soaring costs that can lead to debt and worse, and the emotional risk of a painful crash after the big day's finally over and you have to return to your glamourless everyday life.

You did it because it seemed like the appropriate thing at the time? Oy vey. Where do I start? You can't go through life doing exactly what everyone else around you is doing, no matter how tempting or easy, because the effects can be disastrous when you finally learn to think for yourself and realise you're *not* exactly like everyone else around you. Conformity can be crushing if it leads you to make choices that don't suit your character.

You wanted to have kids? That's no excuse; you can be a fantastic parent in any kind of relationship, so best to be in the relationship that suits both parents the most and keeps them the happiest and most stable so they can focus on their children's needs. It's perfectly possible to separate your marital status from your parental status and make sure that everyone involved is satisfied without compromising your responsibility towards your kids. If you're going to get married do it for yourself and your partner; your children won't thank you for a messy divorce.

You don't want to be alone? Well, newsflash: if you're not happy by yourself you're not going to be happy with anyone else. Before you even start thinking of hitching your wagon to some poor unsuspecting singleton's it would be a wise idea to sort your head out, get to know yourself, find out what – and who – you really want.

You got married to show your commitment? Two words – 'divorce' and 'rate'.

Some of us just aren't capable of committing for life, no matter how normal and appropriate it's deemed to be, so signing up to stick it out until death does its parting act is a recipe for disaster. Divorce is the dark side of marriage, and like marriage itself it can get ugly and messy and dirty. No marriage equals no divorce. That doesn't, of course, save anyone from the possibility of bitter break-ups, but it does mean there's no legislative framework that those break-ups have to limp their sorry way through before they can finally be over. Some of us will be happier and more fulfilled with our partners if we don't formalise and codify our relationships, don't load them up with the extra pressure of having to stay together forever and ever and ever because we said so in the sight of God, our friends, our families and weird uncle Ronnie with the bad teeth.

Some of us will do best on our own, filling our lives with a series of friends and lovers and significant others rather than getting our heads down and pretending to be happy with just the one person for 50 long years. Some people mate for life; others don't. Some mate for life but don't want to be locked into it legally. We are complex, complicated beings and we each operate differently. Assuming that the same thing will make everyone happy is disingenuous and, ironically, contrary to the culture of personal happiness and fulfilment we live in.

Marriage is often viewed as a cold hard unassailable fact, an automatic pact one enters into at some point or another with whoever happens to be the fitting partner at the time, and opting out of it can still seem perverse, difficult, contradictory, a slap in the face for the norms and mores of polite society. This is a harsh consequence to face for people who have jobs, pay taxes, live perfectly reasonable lives and have no desire to step away from or opt out of the majority culture. Not wanting to get married doesn't make you a freaky hippie, or an anarchist dropout, or an antisocial nutcase, but this deeply personal decision can leave you branded with the 'weird' stamp for daring to defy the unshakeable word of convention.

The fact is that what works for one person may not work for another. We don't all attempt to do the same jobs or get fulfilment from the same kinds of fun – why on earth, then, would it make sense for every single human being to organise his or her sexual and emotional life in exactly the same way, just because that's what's been done before? We've managed, in Western culture, to let go of all sorts of other habits that were once the done thing. No one asks to check the bridal sheets for virginal blood any more and few of us marry off our teenage daughters to rich landowners in their 50s. The world has changed and so has the way we engage with it; and yet some of us are still pointlessly attached to the silly anachronism of marriage, a structure without substance that, of itself, no longer adds any value to our lives. Marriage only works when a couple would work out anyway; when they wouldn't, it becomes a legal, financial and emotional burden that they'd be significantly better off without.

Ironically, the creeping irrelevance of marriage is a consequence of the emphasis on marriage as a site of satisfaction rather than social responsibility. The 'love match' has become the normal marital template, and people seldom wed for economic or political reasons. Personal happiness, both within marriage and within other areas of society in wealthy Western Europe and North America, has become a right, something we all deserve, something we're entitled to pursue as far as we can. This trend has seen rocketing divorce rates and also a new twist in the supposed universality of marriage.

We get married now because it's assumed that it will make us happy. All the films and love songs tell us so; it's the fairytale ending that we all want and expect and believe in disguising yet another of those mass delusions that our culture fosters so elegantly. Many of us are finding to our detriment that marriage doesn't make you happy; just the opposite. We're expecting Paris in the Spring and getting Fallujah in the Fall, a war zone constructed on the model of a thousand Mills & Boon novels that has us trapped and panicked. We're making bad choices for bad reasons when we're too young or naïve or hormonal or broody or easily led to question the assumptions and received ideas that push us onto that particular path. Some of us are being clever and waiting until we're a little older and a little surer of our own minds. Some of us are opting out of it altogether, backing away from the convenient fiction that this tired and rigid institution is the only way to find personal fulfilment.

The very insistence on marriage as a place where the individual can be happy has made marriage extraneous, useless, needless. Because if personal happiness is the goal then marriage is just a means to it, a means that's *only useful when it's working*. We can have children outside marriage with no fear of stigma. In-laws are people we get annoyed by at large family dinners rather than a crucial part of a survival network that keeps our clan alive. We depend on our co-workers, not our spouses, for support and aid in the workplace; in most cases we could survive financially just fine on our own (at least until we get married and run up mortgages and wedding debts). Marriage rarely forges useful alliances between families, and if it does, this is a pleasant side-effect rather than an actual purpose. We can even have sex outside of marriage now that contraception is common and we need not fear a plague of unexpected pregnancies and fatherless children destabilising the social fabric.

None of the original purposes of marriage are valid any more, which leaves us only with a strong framework of tradition and expectation versus the great modern belief in our right to personal happiness. And if your happiness can't be found within marriage then all that's left to recommend it is tradition, the weight of the done thing, the usual path, the common response. None of these are good enough motivations to commit to a serious long-term life choice that will, at the end of the day, affect you far more than it'll affect any of the people who'd disapprove of you if you failed to do it.

Marry in haste, the saying goes, and repent at leisure. Or why not avoid the whole sorry mess and not marry at all? Researching this book led me to a number of surprising conclusions. Where I expected open-mindedness or at least interest I found often horror that I'd dare to interrogate the institution of marriage, and a blanket unwillingness to look at the situation with some perspective. I encountered an astonishing amount of faith in the idea of marriage, against all evidence to the contrary. Some might find this romantic. I found it unsettling, and concrete proof of the unshakeable power of generally accepted social structures, no matter how carefully you deconstruct them or illustrate from people's own lives that they're prone to failure.

Many of the people I met confirmed my belief that the institution of marriage, like most things in life, only works well when you *make* it work well. In itself marriage is no curative, nor is it an automatically healthy situation. It can be as screwed up and painful as any casual relationship, with the added angst of legalities to be got through if it all goes horribly wrong. Time and time again the people I interviewed told me that they'd been too young when they'd decided to do it, or they failed to give me comprehensible reasons at all, retreating into a tragically woolly attempt to justify a bad decision that they weren't even sure why they'd made.

Time and time again I realised that the social pressure to settle down is disproportionately huge considering how many other life choices are available for those with the guts and the freedom to try them. I spoke to men and women who'd entered into marriages the way other people get driving licences or lose their virginity, as a generic rite of passage that was inevitable at some point in their future. But it isn't. You can commit to someone and have a healthy and stable life with them without ever needing to translate your relationship into terms the rest of the world can understand. And that's largely what marriage is these days, outside of its legal consequences: a way of framing your life in a language that the world understands, of making yourself explicable and easily categorised so your government and the people around you will know which box to put you in. Which also seems like a fairly flimsy reason for making such an enormous decision.

What it all comes down to is that some things work for some people, other things work for other people. We don't all like Marmite, or country music, or cats, or having sex in the shower. We don't all eat the same things or wear the same things. Some of us cook, some of us order out, some of us are vegetarians, some like their steak bloody. For every human being there is a whole new and diverse set of preferences, prejudices and proclivities. We allow ourselves the freedom to live according to these tastes; we should show the same respect to the way we love. Marriage may be a wonderful institution for some but for others it's a prison sentence, constricting and agonising. Before you go making any big jumps, before you fall too in love with the idea of a sparkly ring and a lot of presents, try to find out which type you are. Because at the end of the day, no matter how much your parents and friends and family and leaders and idols may have to say about it, the people who suffer most when a marriage goes wrong are those who are in it.

Notes

Author's note

1 Stephanie Coontz (2005) *Marriage, A History: How Love Conquered Marriage*, Penguin Books, New York

2 Nina Farewell (2004) *The Unfair Sex: An Exposé of the Human Male for Young Women of All Ages*, Icon Books, Cambridge, p16

Introduction

1 'Weddings at "lowest ever" level', BBC, 21 February 2007, www.bbc.co.uk

2 In the United Kingdom, for example, the Social Justice Policy Group – a think tank headed by former Conservative Party leader Iain Duncan Smith – released a report called *Breakthrough Britain* in July 2007, suggesting a direct link between the collapse of marriage and family values and Britain's social problems. Current Tory leader David Cameron took up his customary spot on the pro-marriage bandwagon, declaring, 'Our support for families and for marriage puts us on the side of the mainstream majority, on the side of a progressive politics, on the side of change that says we can stop social decline, we can fix our broken society, we can and will make this a better place to live for everyone' (speech transcript on

www.conservatives.com, 10 July 2007) – as though ensuring that more of us got married would magically get rid of endemic poverty, racism, sexism, economic inequality and Britain's all-pervasive class system.

3 'Marriage rates continue to slide', BBC, 29 September 2005, www.bbc.co.uk

4 Betty Friedan (1963) *The Feminine Mystique*, WW Norton, New York

5 'Betty Friedan, who ignited cause in *Feminine Mystique*, dies at 85', *New York Times*, 5 February 2006, www.nytimes.com

6 Stephanie Coontz, *Marriage, A History*, p228

7 Stephanie Coontz, *Marriage, A History*, p5

8 Martin King Whyte (1990) *Dating, Mating and Marriage*, Aldine de Gruyter, New York

9 For a clear and concise history of some strands of Mormonism's difficult relationship with polygamy, see Jon Krakauer (2003) *Under the Banner of Heaven: A Story of Violent Faith*, Doubleday, USA.

10 Suzanne Frayser (1985) *Varieties of Sexual Experience: An Anthropological Perspective on Human Sexuality*, HRAF Press, New Haven, p248

11 This lone exception is the Na people of China who are farmers in the Himalayan region. As explained in Dr Cai Hua's influential anthropological text *A Society Without Fathers or Husbands* (MIT Press, Massachusetts, 2001), the Na have nothing comparable to marriage, instead using sibling and family bonds to structure their society. Brothers and sisters live together their entire lives and raise the sisters' children, who are fathered by late-night visits from outsiders with no claim on them. Their incest prohibition is as strong as most societies', and all they really seem to be lacking is a system of in-laws.

12 Amy Kaler (2001) 'Many divorces and many spinsters: marriage as an invented tradition in southern Malawi, 1946–1999',

Journal of Family History, 26

13 Stephanie Coontz, *Marriage, A History*, p31

14 The United States has about 80 teen pregnancies per 1,000. Rather than being in the league of other developed nations it sits alongside Belarus, Bulgaria and Romania. Japan and most Western European countries have 40 per 1,000, while Holland, that hotbed of radicalism with its legal drugs and hookers, has just 12. For more information on the contradictory sexual messages the US Government is throwing at its teens, read Ariel Levy (2005) *Female Chauvinist Pigs: Women and the Rise of Raunch Culture*, Free Press, USA.

15 These days even being royal is no impediment to doing what you damn well please. Crown Prince Haakon of Norway told controversy to get stuffed in 2001 when he married his live-in lover Mette-Marit Tjessem Høiby. Not only had they shacked up before announcing their engagement, she was a commoner. And a single mother. And now she's a Crown Princess. Nice work if you can get it.

16 Interview with the author, 3 May 2007

17 'Marriage is knot too pleasing', *Sun*, 12 April 2007

Chapter One

1 'Marriage in America: the frayed knot', *Economist*, 24 May 2007, www.economist.com

2 It's a commonly accepted urban myth that the Coca-Cola Company invented Santa Claus. The image of Santa as a big fat man in a red-and-white suit was fairly common throughout the United States by the 1920s, some years before illustrator Haddon Sundblom drew the iconic Coke ads that entrenched him in the world's consciousness forever. There can be little doubt, however, that the economic might of the company helped spread his image across the globe.

3 Deirdre O'Siodhachain, 'The practice of courtly love' available

at http://moas.atlantia.sca.org/oak/04/court.htm
4 For those seeking an antidote to the doe-eyed twaddle spouted by most novels with love at their core I suggest F Scott Fitzgerald's *The Beautiful and the Damned*, in which a rich, good-looking young couple marry in a haze of romance, only for each to eventually realise that their spouse is all too depressingly average.
5 Joseph Pequigney (1985) *Such Is My Love: A Study of Shakespeare's Sonnets*, University of Chicago Press, Chicago
6 Michael Bloch (ed) (1988) *Wallis And Edward, Letters 1931–1937: The Intimate Correspondence of the Duke and Duchess of Windsor*, Summit Books, New York
7 George Bernard Shaw (1908) Introduction to *Getting Married*, eBook from Project Gutenberg (www.gutenberg.org)
8 From an appearance in the BBC series *Body Hits* on 4 December 2002
9 'The science of love', ABC News, 30 September 2004, www.abcnews.go.com
10 Andreas Bartels and Semi Zeki (2000) 'Neural basis of romantic love', *NeuroReport*, 2
11 Helen Fisher (2004) *Why We Love: The Nature and Chemistry of Romantic Love*, Henry Holt, USA
12 Quoted in Sam Vaknin (2007) *Malignant Self Love: Narcissism Revisited*, Narcissus, USA
13 'Sex chemistry lasts two years', BBC, 1 February 2006, www.bbc.co.uk
14 'Revealed: the chemistry of love', *Independent on Sunday*, 27 November 2005
15 Interview with the author, 20 February 2007

Chapter Two

1 On 27 July 2005, for example, not long after the 7 July attacks on London, the *Daily Express* trumpeted, 'Bombers are all

spongeing asylum seekers'; this while the identities of two of the bombers were still unknown and it was certain that none of the others were asylum seekers.

2 Refugees and Asylum Seekers Worldwide as of 31 December 2006, US Committee for Refugees and Immigrants, www.refugees.org
3 Afrikaans slang for queer
4 Whether they're immoral too is a question of your personal belief system. For some, the existence of border controls in nations that made their fortunes from slavery, colonialism and genocide is immoral, and marrying someone so they can live in your country is one tiny way that the little guy can strike back at the oppressive global order. This is, however, a topic for a different polemic entirely.
5 1985 survey from the General Accounting Office, the investigative arm of Congress
6 'Sham marriage immigration attempts rise', *The Age*, 28 December 2005, www.theage.com.au
7 Reported on www.workpermit.com, 11 January 2007
8 This humble author is not in the habit of agreeing with politicians wherever possible, working on the basic assumption that anyone who really wants that much power shouldn't be allowed to have it.
9 For non-UK readers, an ASBO is an Anti-Social Behaviour Order, a punishment handed out for anything from letting your dog defecate in the street to hassling your neighbours or vandalising cars. More than this, it's become a class marker in the United Kingdom, tied to images of 'chavs', council estates and working-class white culture.
10 Keynote speech delivered at the Conservative Party spring conference in Wales on 5 March 2007
11 'Blair attacks pro-marriage Tory tax break', *The Times*, 4 March 2007

12 Official government policy generally disapproves of abortion while tolerating it (and even this is under threat in the United States), and frowns on single-parent families. So if a single woman gets pregnant accidentally, what are her options? Get her brothers to organise a shotgun wedding with the guilty party, who's probably a drummer called Terry? Invest in a time machine and go back and tell herself not to have that last Bacardi Breezer?

13 For more on the negative myths surrounding single parenting see Chapter Five.

14 Published in *Journal of Health and Social Behaviour* and quoted in 'Bad marriage may make you sick', *Web MD Medical News*, 29 March 2006, www.webmd.com

15 'Why a bad marriage is worse for women than men', *Monitor on Psychology* 32(11)

16 'Discovering what it takes to live to 100', *New York Times*, 25 December 2001, www.nytimes.com

17 Stephanie Coontz, *Marriage, A History*, p310

Chapter Three

1 J L Austin (1962) *How to Do Things with Words: The William James Lectures Delivered at Harvard University in 1955*, ed J Urmson, Clarendon, Oxford

2 *Stern Review on the Economics of Climate Change*, 30 October 2006, available on www.hm-treasury.gov.uk

3 'Summary for policy makers of the working group two contribution', Intergovernmental Panel on Climate Change, 6 April 2007, available on www.ipcc.ch

4 'Stop shopping . . . or the planet will go pop', *Observer*, 8 April 2007

5 See the award-winning 2004 film *Maria Full of Grace* to put a human face on the complicated situation in this country, or visit the Colombia Support Network (www.colombiasupport.net)

or Amnesty International (www.amnesty.org).

6 'Kenya's flower power', BBC, 5 April 2001, www.bbc.co.uk

7 If you prefer your politics with less anger and more eye candy, have a look at the films *Lord of War*, where Nicolas Cage's arms dealer is paid with diamonds by an African warlord, or *Blood Diamond*, starring Leonardo DiCaprio and set during the Sierra Leonian civil war. Or have a listen to British rapper Ms Dynamite's 'It takes more', a jibe at hip-hop's bling-and-golf-and-Courvoisier consumption culture that points out the deeply ironic link between African deaths and American diamonds.

8 'Attending weddings has its price,' *The Scotsman*, 31 March 2007, www.scotsman.com

9 'The cost of marriage in the UK', British Council Japan, January 2005, www.britishcouncil.org

10 The site is owned by The Wedding Report, a leading provider of statistics and market research for the wedding industry.

11 Available from www.theweddingreport.com

12 'Ka-ching! Wedding price tag nears $30k', CNN, 20 May 2005, money.cnn.com

13 'The cost of a wedding', *Guardian*, 11 February 2002

14 'Here comes the bride – and an overdraft', BBC, 4 April 2005, www.bbc.co.uk

15 'Couples get wedding costs wrong', BBC, 22 July 2005, www.bbc.co.uk

16 If you are having trouble with money, Credit Action offer friendly, useful, non-judgemental advice. See www.creditaction.org.uk for details. Hey, it can happen to all of us. (Except Hugh Hefner. Obviously.)

17 'Debt facts and figures', 1 June 2007, www.creditaction.org.uk, accessed on 31 July 2007

18 From www.moneybasics.co.uk, accessed on 31 July 2007

19 From www.yeartosuccess.com, accessed on 31 July 2007

20 'Fannie, Freddie can buy larger loans in 2005', *USA Today*, 30 November 2004, www.usatoday.com

21 'DCLG confirms house price rise', *Guardian*, 11 June 2007

22 'Celebrity nuptials rekindle love affair with weddings', *Guardian*, 14 October 2002

23 Scientologists are generally secretive about their practices but it is known that one of the religion's more traditional wedding ceremonies involves the use of the word 'girl' instead of the bride's name and her promising to accept her man's fortune 'at its prime and ebb'. Maybe Katie's decision was based on minimal expectation of ebb. Or maybe I'm just an old cynic.

24 That's the same date as the Holmes–Cruise extravaganza, fact fans. And it's also the date of this author's birthday. Coincidence? I think not.

25 'Brides get the blues as the magic wanes', *Observer*, 14 September 2003

26 'Brides get the blues as the magic wanes', *Observer*, 14 September 2003

27 Interview with the author, 3 May 2007

28 'Post-nuptial depression on the rise', *Times of India*, 10 September 2006, timesofindia.indiatimes.com

Chapter Four

1 The classic – if one can use such a positive term for such a horrific situation – example of this is the 1964 murder of New Yorker Kitty Genovese. Returning home in the early hours of the morning, Genovese was attacked and stabbed by Winston Moseley. She screamed for help and her cries were heard by several neighbours. Moseley ran away but returned ten minutes later, systematically searched the area and found the wounded Genovese. He attacked her again and sexually assaulted her, then stole what money she had and left her dying.

A few minutes after the final attack, a witness called the police. Genovese died en route to the hospital. The case caused a ensation, with the *New York Times* reporting that 38 neighbours ignored her death cries. While this is an exaggeration, police did state that at least 12 neighbours heard or witnessed parts of the attack and failed to help her. The reasons most commonly cited for their lack of response were not realising the full extent of the situation, not wanting to get involved and assuming someone else would help. The case is often used by psychologists to illustrate the principles of 'bystander syndrome'.

2 'Conformity and obedience', available from the Social Psychology section of Dr Boeree's website: webspace.ship.edu/cgboer

3 Solomon Asch (1951) 'Effects of group pressure upon the modification and distortion of judgment' in H Guetzkow (ed), *Groups, Leadership and Men*, Carnegie Press, Pittsburgh, Penn. Solomon Asch (1955) 'Opinions and social pressure', *Scientific American*, 193. Solomon Asch (1956) 'Studies of independence and conformity: a minority of one against a unanimous majority', *Psychological Monographs*, 70

4 Richard Adams (1992) 'Relative preferences', *Yale Law Journal*, **102**(1)

5 Social psychology has reached many other interesting conclusions about the tendency to conform; Norwegians, for example, always conform more than the French. Studies in the United States in the 1950s found that black children and white children conformed to about an equal degree, but both conformed more when the group they were in was mostly white than they did when it was mostly black. A sense of alienation from the mainstream, such as defined the mostly middle-class hippie dropouts in the 1960s, drastically decreases the tendency to conform. In tests using Asch's methods conformity is high in Fiji, Hong Kong, Zaire, Zimbabwe and

Ghana and low in France, the Netherlands, the United Kingdom and Germany. This has been explained in terms of collectivist cultures, where the group's well-being is more important than the individual's, in comparison with individualist cultures, where individual achievement is lauded as the primary goal in life. According to this explanation, Europeans are more individualist and therefore less conformist than Americans.

6 Interview with the author, 12 April 2007.

7 Irving L Janis (1972) *Victims of Groupthink*, Houghton Mifflin, Boston, Mass.

8 Stephanie Coontz, *Marriage, A History*, p85

9 Before I upset anyone I'd like to make it clear that I'm well aware of the many measured and tolerant strands of this religion, people who wouldn't dream of forcing their way of life onto anyone else. It's unfortunate that these likeable and altruistic Christians go by the same name as the lunatic fringe comprised of people like the Westboro Baptist Church, which pickets the funerals of American soldiers who died in Iraq with signs reading 'God Hates Fags', because obviously the Lord is killing US servicemen to punish the country for tolerating homosexuality. I'm not making this up.

10 As a non-religious Jew myself I think I'm well qualified to say that there's a fair degree of expectation in my culture that young people will meet someone nice, maybe a doctor, maybe a lawyer, maybe from a nice family, and settle down to make some grandchildren already. Those of us who haven't quite managed it are often viewed with pity or abandoned to the mercy of matchmaking aunts and the living hell of the online dating site J Date.

11 Anita Jain: 'Is arranged marriage really any worse than Craigslist?', *New York Magazine*, www.nymag.com

12 From their website www.stophonourkillings.com

13 United Nations General Assembly Fifty-Seventh Session, Item 104, 'Working towards the elimination of crimes against women committed in the name of honour', 2 July 2002

14 'Campaigner who still weeps for the mother and father who cast her out', *Sunday Times*, 21 January 2007

Chapter Five

1 Published on www.statistics.gov.uk, sourced from Labour Force Surveys of spring 1996 and 2004 and the Office of National Statistics

2 It goes without saying that, again, these caveats apply to the lucky people living in the wealthy first world who have the health care, education, resources and religious freedom to make informed choices. Whether they choose to take advantage of these enormous benefits is another question altogether. The huge percentage of the world's population who live below the poverty line do not often have the luxury of choice; but then they don't often have the luxury of divorce either, or even of unhappiness within a marriage. This particular strand of misery is reserved for those who know they have enough to eat.

3 Published in www.divorcemag.com, sourced from the US Census Bureau, National Centre for Health Statistics, Americans for Divorce Reform, Centres for Disease Control and Prevention, Institute for Equality in Marriage, American Association for Single People, Ameristat and Public Agenda

4 Although religious and governmental emphasis on marriage may not be as powerful as it once was, it is still pervasive, despite what some of us may think. See for example the UK Conservative Party's attempt to 'return' to family values mentioned in Chapter Six.

5 The people I spoke to while researching this book seemed to be split on their opinions about divorce. Some wished their

parents had stayed together so they could have the benefit of some input from the other sex; others wished their parents had split up rather than be drained and lifeless during their childhoods. Some wished their parents had sacrificed more, some less.

6 Interview with the author, 2 February 2007
7 For a more in-depth examination of the costs, consequences and crises of divorce see Chapter Seven.
8 'Divorce makes people miserable for life', *Observer*, 8 January 2006
9 Kathleen Kiernan (1997) 'The legacy of parental divorce: social, economic and demographic experiences in adulthood', CASE Paper No 1
10 'Pre-divorce problems contribute to later difficulties', the Joseph Rowntree Foundation, 30 September 1997, www.jrf.org.uk
11 Steven D Levitt and Stephen J Dubner (2005) *Freakonomics: A Rogue Economist Explores the Hidden Side of Everything*, William Morrow, New York
12 'The big day: UK divorce most common today', *Guardian*, 8 January 2007
13 Interview with the author
14 Statistics sourced from 2000 US Census Bureau of Household and Family Statistics, *New York Times* of 20 May 2001, *State of America's Children Yearbook 2000*, National Survey of America's Families and Stepfamily Association of America
15 'Lone parent benefits "may change"', BBC, 30 January 2007, www.bbc.co.uk
16 'Single mothers, fathers equally successful at raising children', *Ohio State University Research News*, 30 November 1998
17 From the Cardinal's letter to Tony Blair, published on the Catholic Church in England and Wales website, 2 January 2007, www.catholic-ew.org.uk

Chapter Six

1 If you're seriously considering marrying someone you're unsure about just because you don't know if you'll get anyone else, I suggest you sprint to your nearest bookshop or log onto Amazon as fast as your little fingers can type and buy a yourself a copy of Emily Dubberley's *I'd Rather Be Single Than Settle: Satisfied Solitude and How To Achieve It*, also published by Vision. There is a whole world out there that doesn't involve being part of a couple. Find it.

2 That's Birmingham in the English West Midlands, not Birmingham, Alabama, USA.

3 This is not the place for a dissection of the backlash against feminism, but let me say briefly that this once-noble movement has been discredited with incredible skill, to the point where every time it's mentioned otherwise sensible women shy away in horror from images of unshaven dungaree-clad yoghurt-knitting FemiNazis peddling their brand of loony left hate speak in allotments and gardens across the civilised world. The figure of the feminist has been transformed in the popular imagination from serious political crusader, sometimes feared, sometimes hated, but always potent, to a caricature of the bitter hag who hates men because she can't get one. It's a far more effective tactic for removing a political movement's teeth than demonising it – turn it into a comic character and watch it lose its bite. For an effective way to reclaim the term and its history, see the Fawcett Society's 'This is what a feminist looks like' campaign at www.fawcettsociety.org.uk.

4 'Forever pregnant', *Washington Post*, 16 May 2006, www.washingtonpost.com

5 Think I'm being excessive? Don't forget that the Nazis, those careful architects of racial statehood, insisted that young women had a patriotic duty to be physically healthy because

their main purpose was the bearing of children for the Volk. They imposed tax penalties for remaining single and offered loans to young married couples and subsidies for childbearing.

6 'Older, and somehow wider', *Observer Woman* magazine, 11 February 2007

7 The lucky few get to hold on to their magnetism way past this sell-by date. Sean Connery was voted Sexiest Man of the Century by this same *People* magazine in 1999 – when he was 68. I challenge you to find a female celebrity in the English-speaking world who's still considered a viable siren in her late 60s. (Many European countries have a more appreciative attitude to women over 40. Unfortunately their cultural influence tends to be country-specific, without the wide influence of Hollywood.)

8 'Teri Hatcher: I was sexually abused', *Daily Mail*, 9 March 2006

Chapter Seven

1 Anne probably wished she hadn't been so supportive of her admirer's grand marital plans when, in 1536, he had her accused of witchcraft, adultery and incest, and beheaded. Which is just so much quicker than divorce.

2 YouGov/Sunday Times marriage survey, fieldwork 24 – 30 November 2006, published 14 January 2007, www.timesonline.co.uk

3 www.divorceuk.com, accessed 20 April 2007

4 'Divorce rate highest since 1996', BBC, 31 August 2005, www.bbc.co.uk

5 'To avoid divorce, move to Massachusetts', *New York Times*, 14 November 2004, www.nytimes.com

6 'Born again less likely to co-habit, just as likely to divorce', The Barna Group, 6 August 2001, www.barna.org

7 'Mamma's boys fuel Italy's soaring divorce rates', *Guardian*, 12 November 2006, www.guardian.co.uk

8 'Calling it quits: women act early but men take ages', *The Australian*, 1 March 2007, theaustralian.news.com.au
9 From www.stats.gov.nz, accessed on 2 May 2007
10 From www.divorcerate.org, accessed on 2 May 2007
11 'Divorce, Japanese style', Japan Zone, www.japan-zone.com
12 '80 per cent of marriages in Russia end up in divorce', *Pravda*, www.english.pravda.ru
13 'The real cost of divorce', BBC, 25 October 2006, www.bbc.co.uk
14 'Rising cost of divorce', Sky News, 13 December 2006, news.sky.com
15 'Sorry, I don't love you any more – but how can we afford to divorce?', *Guardian*, 18 June 2006
16 'Counsellors and divorce lawyers rejoice – a long queue of new and wealthy victims is heading your way', *Guardian*, 22 December 2005
17 'It's personal for a top NYC divorce lawyer', *New York Sun*, 17 May 2005, www.nysun.com
18 No, really. If you don't believe me have a look at www.DivorcePartyPlanner.com, the website for Christine Gallagher's bestseller of the same name. Testimonials range from 'My divorce party brought much needed closure to a horrible time in my life' to 'My sister invited lots of single men and I found out that there is life after divorce'. Or you could head to Vegas for a bespoke divorce party that's every bit as much fun as your stag or hen weekend. Any minute now, Hallmark will be doing 'happy divorce' cards complete with sickly rhyming poems about caterpillars and butterflies.
19 Bartha's is a tragic tale. There are many others in a similar mode that are vindictive rather than suicidal and make for amusing pub conversation. In March 2007, for example, a German mason decided to take his imminent divorce into his own hands, measuring his home carefully, chainsawing it into

perfect halves and removing his section with a forklift.

20 Norwich Union Cost of Divorce survey, quoted in 'Rising cost of divorce', Sky News, 13 December 2006, news.sky.com, and 'It's personal for a top NYC divorce lawyer', *New York Sun*, 17 May 2005, www.nysun.com

21 Interview with the author, 2 February 2007

22 While the ensuing scandal effectively derailed his career and appalled sophisticated Europe and America, in 1957 marrying a blood relative in her teens was nothing unusual for a boy from rural Louisiana. Interrogated about his questionable choice in women, a gazumped Jerry Lee responded, 'But I married her, didn't I?' And after all that the marriage still didn't last; Myra divorced him in 1970.

23 Just in case Miss Gabor's love life wasn't complex enough, her husband, Prince Frederic von Anhalt, was one of men who claimed paternity of Anna Nicole Smith's daughter Dannielynn after Smith died of an overdose and left her baby a potential goldmine. Curiouser and curiouser . . .

24 'Malaysian ties knot for 53rd time', BBC, 6 October 2004, www.bbc.co.uk

25 Craig Glenday (ed) *Guinness World Records 2007*, Bantam Books, England

26 For our US friends, wankered in UK parlance refers to being drunk or high rather than anything more sordid.

27 'Gay in SA: to wed or not?', BBC, 14 November 2006, www.bbc.co.uk

28 Just two months and two weeks after getting hitched, South Africa's first gay divorcees were making headlines across the country. Kenneth Henning-Hattingh, 28, and Jaco Johan Henning-Hattingh, 29, were married on 2 January 2007, two months after the Civil Union Act was signed into law. The break-up was amicable but it injected a harsh note of early-days realism into the romantic dream of perfect same-sex

partnership.

29 'Counsellors and divorce lawyers rejoice – a long queue of new and wealthy victims is heading your way', *Guardian*, 22 December 2005

30 'Counsellors and divorce lawyers rejoice – a long queue of new and wealthy victims is heading your way', *Guardian*, 22 December 2005

31 'Gay pacts go straight as lovers get cold feet over ties of marriage', *The Times*, 2 December 2006

About the author

Nicky Falkof is a freelance writer and editor and is studying towards a PhD in humanities. She lives in Brighton and is, unsurprisingly, single. *Ball and Chain* is her first book.